Official
Know-It-All
Guide™

ONLINE
INVE$TING

Your Absolute, Quintessential, All You Wanted to Know, Complete Guide

William M. Frantz

Frederick Fell Publishers, Inc.

Fell's Official Know-It-All Guide

Frederick Fell Publishers, Inc.

2131 Hollywood Boulevard, Suite 305

Hollywood, Florida 33020

954-925-5242

e-mail: fellpub@aol.com

Visit our Web site at www.fellpub.com

Library of Congress Cataloging-in-Publication Data

Frantz, William M., 1965-
    Online investing: your absolute, quintessential, all you wanted to know, complete guide / William M. Frantz.
      p. cm. -- (Fell's official know-it-all guide)
    Includes bibliographical references.
    ISBN 0-88391-061-6
    1. Electronic trading of securities. 2. Investments--Computer network resources. I. Title.II.Series.

    HG4515.95 .F73 2001
    332.63'2'02854678--dc21   00-061744

Interior Design by: JABEZ and Carey Jacobs

Acknowledgement & Dedication

I want to acknowledge the loving
support of my parents
Bill and Midge throughout
and I wish to dedicate this book to
my son Johnny.

CONTENTS

CONTENTS

CONTENTS

PREFACE

Fell's Official Know-It-All Guide to Online Investing is your 21ST century investor's guide to Wall Street. This book provides the leading edge of 21ST century investment combining a traditional investor's guide with a cyber guide to online investments and trading. The 21ST century investor's guide to Wall Street is for anyone interested in investing in the 21ST century.

The book is also educational as it is intended to provide the investor and industry professional with a through understanding of 21ST century Wall Street, all viewed through the Internet as a learning resource. In order to accomplish this, Fell's Official Know-It-All Guide to Online Investing provides a fully illustrated guided tour of Wall Street. By the final Chapter, the investor or industry professional emerges with a strong understanding of the finance and investment side of the Internet. The reader also emerges with the tools necessary to make sound, effective investment choices and decisions in the 21ST century.

This book is structured and presented in an easy-to-use format that enables someone who has never gone online before to surf the Web with ease. Once online, the investor or industry professional will be able to take full advantage of the awesome power of the internet. Industry professional will also find this book suitable for making recommendations to clients.

If you already surf online, you will be pleasantly surprised to find very useful financial websites that you never knew existed and that would have taken hundreds of hours to find. This Guide is designed to allow you to quickly reference and review websites relevant to your surfing needs and to choose those that are of interest in the fasted way possible.

INTRODUCTION

The 21ST century is here and Wall Street is deciding how business is to be carried out in the New Millennium. As we all know, the stock market is lightning fast to respond to even the most subtle factors and once a trend is established it is often followed by millions of investors. The big winners are those with those the foresight and the knowledge to back sound investment choices.

Investment success in the 21ST century, as in the previous millennium, will come to those who can anticipate major changes in Wall Street before others. The technology of the Internet will provide the information and tools that investment leaders will utilize to leave all others behind in cyber dust.

Chapter One

– WELCOME TO –

21st CENTURY WALL STREET

Knowledge empowers. An investor with knowledge is far more likely to make sound investment decisions. This Guide will empower you to be more knowledgeable when you work with a broker or invest online by yourself. In order to bring investors into the new investment era, the Guide emphasizes online investing and provides investors with reviews of many financial websites. Why is this so important?

The World Wide Web is an incredible knowledge-based resource. Successful navigation of the Internet will help you keep pace with the lightening speed of 21st Century investing. Wall Street has changed tremendously because of this unbelievably fast paced information technology. The Internet, with its speed and power, will continue to break new ground. Those who are adept at navigating and utilizing the Internet as a tool for investing will make logical and informed investment choices. They will reap the rewards that follow sound investment decisions.

With *Fell's Official Know-It-All Guide to Online Investing*, even an Investor without any knowledge of the Internet will be able to go online to take full advantage of the wealth of valuable investment information, products and services available on the World Wide Web. Once online, even an Investor who has never used the Internet will become an empowered 21st Century Investor.

There are literally thousands of investment related websites on the Internet. This book presents key websites that are concise, well presented, informative and easy-to-use.

The *Know-It-All Guide to Online Investing* is also an excellent source of information for securities industry professionals and financial planning professionals.

Beyond a mere list of websites, **Fell's Official Know-It-All Guide to Online Investing** *is structured to bring investors online and provide everyone with fully illustrated premiere websites.*

Many investors trade stocks, purchase bonds, mutual funds, annuities and options, without understanding the industry. Wall Street is the home of the stock market where big brokerage firms invest our money every day. Wall Street is more than just a street. It is the heart of the American economy.

One of the most significant changes ever to hit Wall Street is the Internet. A significant percentage of the investing public conduct business on it. This certainly was not the choice of brokerage firms who scrambled to adjust to the rapid pace of online investing.

Fell's Official Know-It-All Guide to Online Investing describes what Wall Street looks like online and how it will function online. The guide also addresses the issue of how to be successful trading online. The computer age is upon us. For a large number of investors, computers are still a mysterious device. If you fall into this category, Chapters 1 through 4 will guide you to computer literacy and prepare you to surf for the wealth of financial information available on the Internet. Computers and the Internet are key components in the structure of Wall Street. Wait, that is not all. When the White House was destroyed by fire during the War of 1812, it was later rebuilt and then rebuilt again, with Presidents and architects always adhering to the original structure and the builder's original intent. However, with each new President the interior and decor changed. Some even made structural changes to the exterior, yet all kept the traditional structure in mind when doing so. Like the White House,

Wall Street is a part of traditional Americana. The buildings on Wall Street will continue to look as they have since they were built, for quite some time. However, the internal workings of Wall Street and how business is transacted has completely changed. When we take our 21st century investor and add the computer and the Internet to the scenario we have the largest technological change ever to hit Wall Street. This new technology has created immense opportunities for those who understand and utilize it.

There is even more. What about those old stock exchanges--the American Stock Exchange and the New York Stock Exchange? The exchanges will continue to do business as they have, but with one exception. The exchanges, and there are far more than two, have already adapted to the Internet revolution. They are already online and offer far more information than they ever have before. This is something definitely worth exploring. Even Wall Street regulators have adapted to the changes. Now you can contact the Securities & Exchange Commission and other regulators online. This has never happened before.

What about the Wall Street Journal? For decades it has been the main source for financial news. Now the Wall Street Journal is online, as is Barron's, BusinessWeek, Forbes, Fortune and many others. All offer information online that previously you could only obtain by purchasing a newspaper or business magazine. The trick is, online news and magazine articles are constantly updated to keep you immediately up to date on the latest business news and trends.

What about investments? You would be amazed to see what the Internet has to offer in terms of financial analysis and research. If you enjoy charts and graphs, you will want to check out online financial analysis and research services that are available. This will be especially advantageous to an industry professional or investor who performs his own research.

This is how the internals of Wall Street have changed. In the 21st century investors will purchase cyber-stock, high tech stock, bonds, mutual funds, CDs, annuities, options, futures and commodities on the World Wide Web.

The biggest change in Wall Street is how business is carried out. Many brokerage firms, like American Express, have adapted to the changes in Wall Street by offering online brokerage services. The biggest change in Wall Street is how business is carried out. Many brokerage firms, like American Express, have adapted to the changes in Wall Street by offering online brokerage services. Over five years ago no one would have believed that investors would be conducting their own trades, by computer, on the Internet. Millions of investors are taking advantage of the Internet and are opening online accounts. Times have changed, and they will continue to do so.

21st Century Wall Street is not that different in appearance from what it was in the 20th Century, however, the infrastructure is pure 21st Century.   Let's begin our cyber-tour of 21st Century Wall Street.

Chapter Two

WHAT YOU NEED
TO GO ONLINE

There are a few components that you need to go online -- *a monitor, a processor, a built in CD-ROM drive, a built in modem, and a mouse.* Unless you know a fair amount about computers, it is probably best to choose a computer that comes with a monitor. In terms of the CD-ROM and modem, do not under any circumstance purchase a computer without these accessories. A modem is necessary to connect to an online service provider like America Online. If your machine does not have a built-in modem, then you will need to search for a modem that is compatible with the computer you have purchased. This will delay your ability to get online.

If you want to run software in the 21st Century, you need a CD-ROM driver in your computer to load the software. This is also true for printer drivers that require CD-ROM capacity to load the drivers necessary for the computer to interact with the printer.

The modem has an outlet for inputting the telephone line to the computer. If you do not designate a second line for your computer with the telephone company, you will not be able to call in or out on the telephone, while you are online. If you believe this will be an inconvenience call the telephone company and have a second line designated for the modem.

You can also go online with a cable feed through your local cable company. If you choose this option, you will not have to utilize the telephone to go online. I discuss going online with cable toward the end of this Chapter.

You will also need a printer if you intend to print information from the Internet. We look at printers after our discussion of computers.

COMPUTERS   As we previously discussed, you will definitely need a computer to go online. I have compiled a solid list of computer manufacturers from the Internet. We will look at a number of these companies and the computers they offer.

You can make purchases directly over the Internet. Nevertheless, this section of the Guide should allow you to understand the main IBM compatible computers that are out there, as well as their competitor, Apple Computer. It is beyond the scope of this book to list all of the products offered by each manufacturer. Instead, I encourage a person seeking a computer to review the computer companies I have listed, and then further explore the web site of the company, or companies, you find are best suited for your computing needs. You can shop factory direct, or you may go to your local computer store, once you have reviewed the computers featured here, and ask as many questions as you can conjure up. You should then be ready to choose the best machine for your needs. I recommend a desktop Personal Computer (PC) over a laptop because the personal computer's screen is larger and easier to read than the laptop's. Feature for feature the personal computer is also less expensive.

IBM COMPATIBLE COMPUTERS

IBM compatible computers vary in terms of components, as we will see, however, they are generally compatible with each other in terms of the basic operating system, Microsoft Windows.

Microsoft Windows is an operating system designed by Microsoft, Bill Gates' company. Microsoft Windows currently comes in three versions: Windows 95, Windows 98, and the newest version, Windows 2000. Older IBM compatibles run Windows 95 and the newest will run Windows 98 or Windows 2000. Internet Explorer is a feature of Windows that permits you to surf the Internet. IBM compatibles are generally sold with Windows already installed. If not you can contact Microsoft Windows @ www.microsoft.com.

The Microsoft Windows operating system is utilized by IBM compatible computers. Microsoft Windows enables IBM compatible computers to share the same software. This means that if you own an IBM compatible computer, for example a Compaq computer, you can purchase the same computer programs

as a person who owns a Dell computer, assuming both are running Microsoft Windows. The reason is if both computers use the Microsoft Windows operating system, the software is designed to run on the Microsoft Windows operating system.

If you have a colleague who owns a Compaq computer running Microsoft Windows and he recommends a software package, for example, Pro Suite 2000 by Megaresearch.com, you can purchase that same software and run it on your Dell computer. On the other hand if you own an Apple computer, discussed later in this chapter, you will have to purchase the Macintosh version of the program to run the same software.

Compaq is a Fortune Global 100 company, and is the second largest computer company in the world. Compaq is also the largest global supplier of personal computers. Compaq offers a number of computer products for the home and business including desktops and laptops. Desktops range from the mid $1,200 dollar range to a little more than $1,500. The Deskpro EN Series offers 22.6 Gigabytes (GB) of memory, and a host of configurations to choose from, Figure 2-1.

Compaq @
www.compaq.com

Figure 2-1

Dell @ *www.dell.com*

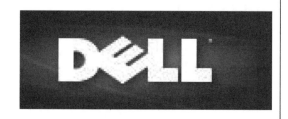

Figure 2-2

    Dell is one of the world's leading direct computer systems companies, with 33,200 employees in 34 countries around the globe. Dell was founded in 1984 with only $1,000. Dell became a fortune 500 company in 1992. Dell offers a complete Pentium III system for $999. Dell also offers Notebooks and accessories. Desktops can be purchased for as low as $899, Figure 2-2.

Fujitsu @ *www.fujitsu.com*

FUJITSU THE POSSIBILITIES ARE INFINITE

Figure 2-3

Fujitsu was established from the Communications Division of Fuji Electric Co., Ltd. in June of 1935. Fujitsu is a manufacturer and seller of software and services, computers and information processing platforms, telecommunications systems, semiconductors and electronic devices. Fujitsu employs 188,000 worldwide.

Fujitsu views their personal computers as the standard workhorse of multinational businesses, trusted for flexible design and reliable operation. Fujitsu's computers come in three types: notebooks, desktops and pen tablet, Figure 2-3.

Gateway @ *www.gateway.com*

Figure 2-4

Gateway began operation in 1985, and is now traded on the New York Stock Exchange. Gateway employs 18,000 people worldwide. Gateway is headquartered in San Diego, California.

Gateway offers desktop personal computers ranging in price from $799 to nearly $4,000. The Gateway Astro sells for $799. It has an Intel Celeron Processor, and a 4.3 Gigabyte Ultra ATA hard drive, Figure 2-4.

Hewlett Packard @ *www.pandi.hp.com*

— *Figure 2-5* —————————

Hewlett Packard (HP) was founded in 1939. Hewlett Packard employs 83,200 world wide and has 70 divisions throughout the globe. Hewlett Packard is a leading global provider of computing, Internet and Intranet solutions, services and communication products.

Hewlett Packard has three series' of personal computers: 4000, 6000 and 8000. The 4000 series consists of the 4563Z and the 4553Z. Hewlett Packard's Pavilion 4563Z PC retails for around $798. The Hewlett Packard 4553ZPC costs $1,098.

The higher the series number the more expensive the computer, Figure 2-5.

IBM @ *www.ibm.com*

Figure 2-6

International Business Machines Corporation (IBM) was formed in 1911. IBM stock is listed on the New York Stock Exchange and other exchanges across the United States. IBM employs 291,067 people.

IBM offers a number of computers, and as the name implies, IBM's primary focus is business machines. An example of this is the PC 300 GL. The PC 300 GL is reasonably priced at $939.00 and a monthly installment plan is also offered. Monitors are sold separately, Figure 2- 6.

SONY *computing* (sony electronics (sony online

Sony @ *www.sony.com*

Figure 2- 7

Sony, based in New York City, is a subsidiary of Sony Corporation headquartered in Tokyo. Sony Corporation is a leading manufacturer of audio, video, communications and information technology products for the consumer and professional markets. Sony employs 177,000 worldwide, Figure 2-7.

Contact
Apple @ *www.store.apple.com*

Figure 2-8

Apple Computer is the main competitor to IBM and the IBM compatible computers listed above. Apple computers carry a different operating system than the IBM compatibles. Apple computers also require software designed for Macintosh. Software designed for Windows will not run on an Apple computer, and vice versa. You can surf the Internet just as easily with an Apple computer as you can with IBM compatibles.

Apple currently sells the iMac ($999), the Power Mac G4 ($1599), the iBook ($1,599) and the PowerBook G3 ($2,499). Surf Apple's website to discover the features of their models, Figure 2-8.

PRINTERS

In terms of printers, it is very important to choose a printer with the capability to print chart information from the Internet, not just text. Having a certain amount of experience with using printers, I only recommend two printers manufacturers: Hewlett Packard and Epson.

Contact
Epson *@ www.epson.com*

Figure 2-9

Epson has a history that spans more than 100 years, with a heritage that began in watchmaking and led to the invention of the world's first quartz watch. In the early 1960's Seiko Epson was established to develop crystal chronometers and printing timers for official timekeeping at the 1964 Tokyo Olympics. Four years later Epson introduced a commercially successful printer mechanism. The rest is history.

Epson sells a number of ink-jet printers from the Epson Stylus Color 440 to the Epson Stylus Photo 700, Figure 2-9

Contact
Hewlett Packard
@www.pandi.hp.com

figure 2-10.

Hewlett Packard printers are excellent. Hewlett Packard sells both black & white and color printers. Color printers also print in black & white. Hewlett Packard printers vary widely in price from ink jet to laser jet printers. Laser jet printers are generally more expensive than ink jets. The Hewlett Packard DeskJet 970C Series is an example of a reasonably priced Hewlett Packard printer, $399. As Hewlett Packard is a premiere printer manufacturer, their prices are often more than other brands. Shop Hewlett Packard's website, Figure 2-10.

23

Chapter Three

CHOOSING AN
INTERNET SERVICE

In the world of the Internet bigger means better technical support and solid rates. Bigger also means more people are utilizing the service and this could slow down surfing speed.

ONLINE SERVICE PROVIDERS

Contact
AOL @www.aol.com

Figure 3-1.

America Online (AOL) was founded in 1985, and is based in Dulles, Virginia. AOL operates two worldwide Internet services, American Online, with more than 20 million members, and CompuServe, with more than 2.2 million subscribers, several leading Internet brands including Netscape Navigator, and Communicator browsers. AOL offers unlimited monthly access for as low as $9.95, and up to $21.95, depending upon options selected, Figure 3-1.

Contact
AT&T WorldNet *@ www.att.com*

Figure 3-2.

AT&T owns AT&T WorldNet, an Internet service provider. AT&T offers unlimited monthly access for as low as $14.95, Figure 3-2.

Contact
CompuServe *@ www.compuserve.com*

Figure 3-3

CompuServe was founded in 1969 as a computer timesharing service in Columbus, Ohio. CompuServe was the first to offer e-mail. CompuServe broke new ground in 1980 by being the first online service to offer real-time chat online. Since February 1998 CompuServe has been a wholly owned subsidiary of AOL. CompuServe's price for unlimited monthly access is $24.95, Figure 3-3.

Contact
MCI WorldCom @ *www.mciworld.com*

Figure 3-4

MCI WorldCom operates in more than 65 countries and is a provider of local, long distance, international and Internet services. MCI WorldCOM Internet offers internet service at $16.95 for local access, with 24-hour toll-free online technical support, Figure 3-4.

Contact
Mindspring@www.mindspring.com

Figure 3-5

MindSpring began in early 1994 offering their online service to 20 people. MindSpring is now traded on NASDAQ. MindSpring offers unlimited Internet service for $19.95, Figure 3-5.

Contact
Prodigy Internet @ www.prodigy.com

Figure 3-6

Prodigy Internet provides direct, nationwide access to the Internet. Prodigy's digital 56kbps network offers members faster connections and delivers faster page downloads. Prodigy provides an access network covering approximately 750 cities in all 50 states allowing 85 percent of the United States population to access Prodigy's services with a local telephone call. Prodigy offers 250 free hours in your first month with unlimited usage for $19.95 thereafter, Figure 3-6.

FREE INTERNET SERVICE PROVIDERS

Contact
Address.com @ *www.address.com*

Figure 3-7

Address.com is a free Internet service provider based in Southern California. It provides free Internet and free e-mail, Figure 3-7.

Contact
Blue Light.com @ *www.bluelight.com*

Figure 3-8

Blue Light.com is a discount-shopping site partnered with K mart. Blue Light.com offers free Internet service, Figure 3-8.

Contact
dotNow @ *www.dotnow.com*

Figure 3-9

dotNow provides free Internet access, Figure 3-9.

Contact
Contact **Freei.net** @ *www.freeinet.com*

Figure 3-10

Freei.net was founded in 1998 as advertising based free Internet service. It also provides free service, Figure 3-10.

Contact
The Free-PC Network @ *www.free-pc.com*

Figure 3-11

The Free-PC Network The Free-PC Network began in February 1999. In November of 1999 Free-PC merged with eMachines, a new personal computer company, Figure 3-11. Free-PC internet service is at no charge.

Contact
iFreedom.com @ *www.ifreedom.com*

Figure 3-12

iFreedom.com provides complete, easy to use free premium Internet access, Figure 3-12.

Contact
Juno @ *www.juno.com*

Figure 3-13.

Juno provides both basic free Internet access, as well as a premium service for $9.95/month, Figure 3-13.

Contact
Net Zero @ *www.netzero.com*

Figure 3-14 ——————

Net Zero began in October 1998. NetZero is a new Internet service that provides consumers with free and easy access to the Internet. NetZero provides consumers with unlimited Internet access, e-mail and navigational tools to enhance their online experience, all for free. You can join Net Zero by downloading Net Zero, Figure 3-14.

CABLE INTERNET PROVIDERS

Internet service providers access the Internet through the telephone. If you do not want to tie up your phone line and are looking for speed, try your local cable company to see if they provide the Internet via cable feed. This gives you high tech performance at a higher price. But it may be well worth the extra cost.

Chapter Four

WEB SURFING

Once you have hooked up to a server and are online, you can surf the World Wide Web (WWW). Surfing is just another term for searching the Internet.

The Internet is a worldwide connection of more than 10 million computers and 45,000 networks that follow the Internet Protocol. The Internet Protocol was invented for the U.S. Department of Defense Advanced Research Projects Agency (ARPA). The Internet can communicate with any user regardless of their location.

The World Wide Web is a networked hypertext system that allows documents to be shared over the Internet. Hypertext is a word that refers to linking of texts. The links give the text an added dimension, which is why it is called hyper.

Every registered user on the Internet has an e-mail address. E-mail permits you to communicate with other people who have e-mail without speaking on the telephone. E-mail might be a useful way to communicate with your stockbroker or financial advisor. Let's get online.

To go online you select the icon for your Internet service provider. Once you have made this selection you need to choose a search engine to search for websites that interest you.

There are a number of search engines you can use to surf the web. Each one is different. I will illustrate some of the more popular search engines and show you how to conduct a search. You can then choose the engine that is best suited to your surfing needs.

Contact
About.Com @ *www.About.Com*

Figure Figure 4-1

About.Com starts with a simple design. Each site at About.Com is overseen by an Expert Guide; a company certified subject specialist. Each targeted, topic-specific site provides an Internet directory. Each site is devoted to a single topic allowing the Guide to focus on an area of expertise. About.Com is based in New York City. When searching the web for mutual funds, About.Com returns with a list of mutual funds sites that you can browse. Clicking onto a site leads us to an About.Com expert guide. You can continue to search About.Com or proceed to another search engine, Figure 4-1.

Contact
Excite @ *www.excite.com*

Figure 4-2

Excite is another search engine that allows you to click onto stock quotes and business news. Using the words "stock quotes" as a search topic, the search engine Excite goes to money & investing. Under the word "investing" another screen appears. You can continue your search using variety of words until you find an area of interest, Figure 4-2.

Contact
Google @ *www.google.com*

Figure 4-3

Google is relatively new search engine, with headquarters in Mountain View, California. It was founded in 1998. Google provides its technologies to customers on its Google Web Search and Google Site Search services.

Using the word "stock market," Google responded with the NASDAQ stock market and other websites. If we click onto "NASDAQ," Google brings us the NASDAQ website. You can then return to the other websites or search again with another search term, Figure 4-3.

Contact
GoTo.Com @ *www.goto.com*

Figure 4-4

GoTo.Com began in 1997 and is based in Pasadena, California. GoTo.Com is a search result oriented search engine which reduces irrelevant information from search results. GoTo.Com matches consumers with advertisers by reducing irrelevant information.Using the term "bonds," GoTo.Com responds with E*Trade: comprehensive bond center. We can continue to search the E*Trade sites or continue on to another website or search engine, Figure 4-4.

Contact
HotBot @ *www.hotbot.com*

Figure 4-5

HotBot is owned by Wired Digital. Wired Digital creates a range of online products that help people put emerging technologies to use in their personal and professional lives. HotBot began in 1996 and has been touted in web search engine reviews.

Using the term "online trading," HotBot responded with the websites including DATEK Online. Choosing "DATEK Online," HotBot brings us to the website for DATEK Online, an online trading company. DATEK's website can be further examined or we can go to another search engine, Figure 4-5.

Contact
LookSmart @
www.looksmart.com

Figure 4-6

LookSmart search engine provides a number of categories for easy searching including a section called stocks & portfolio.

Using the term "stockbrokers," LookSmart returns with a number of websites including stockbrokers at your fingertips. With this search we find an example of an online article, Figure 4-6.

Contact
Netscape @ *www.netscape.com*

Figure 4-7

Netscape offers Salomon Smith Barney stock quotes, e-business basics, and lots of other features including the weather.

Using the word "stock," Netscape provides a number of websites, including the NYSE- New York Stock Exchange website listing. This choice leads us to the NYSE website. The NYSE website will be discussed in Chapter 5, Figure 4-7.

Contact
Yahoo! @ *www.yahoo.com*

Figure 4-8

Yahoo! is a very well developed and popular search engine. The business & economy section of this engine includes a site on finance and investment. Click on "finance and investment" and a number of sub-websites appear. These sub-websites can also be accessed. For example, we can choose investment picks using the term "annuities" and Yahoo! comes up with annuities online, Figure 4-8. We will explore annuities in Chapter 14.

Chapter Five

STOCK EXCHANGES ONLINE

OPTIONS & STOCK EXCHANGES A stock exchange provides a liquid open market for buying and selling shares of publicly owned companies. Closely regulated by the Securities and Exchange Commission (SEC), stock exchanges play a pivotal role in the nation's economy by facilitating the capital-raising process. When a company raises funds to support its growth by selling ownership interests, that is, shares in itself, to the investing public, those shares are listed and traded on America's stock exchanges.

Contact
AMEX @ *www.amex.com*

Figure 5-1

The American Stock Exchange In 1860 the initial steps were taken for the formation of the American Stock Exchange. During the 1990's, AMEX introduced wireless, hand-held terminals on the Trading Floor, a wireless voice technology system to facilitate internal broker communications and the AMEX Data Link digital information delivery service for member firms. AMEX also developed a fully automated AMEX Options Display Book and an Equity Display Book.

The AMEX website offers the following sub sites: market activity, portfolio tracking, equity and index options, index shares, and other options such as IPO's, earnings, and investor resources. You can search each of these subwebsites by clicking the appropriate section of the main website, Figure 5-1.

Contact
the **BSE** @ *www.bostonstock.com*

Figure 5-2

   The Boston Stock Exchange (BSE) began in the 1830's when Bostonians were looking for new ways to invest the wealth they had earned through shipping, banking and insurance. Today, the BSE trades more than 2,000 of the most active U.S. stocks in competition with other exchanges. The BSE also handles trades in 150 securities that are traded either exclusively on the BSE or jointly on another exchange. The BSE is owned by 200 members whose ownership is represented by seats on the exchange.

   Although you cannot trade directly on the exchange, the BSE is part of the Intermarket Trading System (ITS). With ITS, before making a trade, brokers on

the BSE floor can view the current bids and offers for specific stock at every exchange in the country, enabling brokers to determine the best price available. Once a trade is executed on the BSE, or any other Exchange, the information is fed into the national quote system, and becomes part of the consolidated quote tape (ticker tape) you see running across your television screen on business channels. The BSE website has a listing for companies. Under this listing you can click "listed companies" and a sub-search engine appears to enable you to determine if a company is listed on the BSE. If you click on "traded securities," you can search the sub search engine for a particular stock. In either case, you can download lists of companies or stock traded on the BSE.

If you go to the membership section of the BSE website, you can view the BSE membership list with a click. There is also a section of the website covering news & publications, which includes BSE annual reports, Figure 5-2.

Contact
the CBOE @ *www.cboe.com*

Figure 5-3

The Chicago Board Options Exchange was founded in 1973. The CBOE created standardized listed stock options. Prior to 1973, options were traded on an unregulated basis, without adherence to fair and orderly markets.Today, CBOE accounts for more than 51 percent of all U.S. options trading, and 91 percent of all index options trading.

The CBOE order routing system handles more than 85 percent of public customer orders. Instead of the old-fashioned use of hand written cards for trading, CBOE market makers now trade with the assistance of 19oz hand-held computers. 30 percent of public customer orders are now executed on a system known as the Retail Automatic Execution System (RAES).

In most instances the buy and sell orders submitted by customer must be 20 options contracts or less and the premium for the option contract must be below $10. Exceptions include, but are not limited to, options on the Dow Jones Industrial Average, where up to 50 options' contracts are executable on RAES.

To learn about CBOE investor protection you can click "OCC & Investor Protection," on the CBOE Home Page. On the CBOE Home Page you can also click on "quotes." For example, the S&P 500 and the CBOE website, will return with an online option quotation sub search engine. The CBOE website has other search features, which include products, traders' tools, education and direct links. Under direct links, you can find information on new investors, market data, market statistics, strategies and a symbol director. Under contents you can discover information about seat market information, news announcements and investor services, Figure 5-3. Options will be discussed in Chapter 15.

Contact
The **CHX** @
www.chicagostockex.com

The
Chicago
Stock Exchange

Figure 5-4

The Chicago Stock Exchange opened for trading on May 15, 1882. Today, The CHX has more than 4000 issues available for trading. 1998 was a record-breaking year with more than nine billion shares traded and 16 million trades executed. The total value of these transactions was more than $298 billion. The CHX is the second largest U.S. stock exchange.

ON the CHX Home Page you will find a number of choices including daily volume, listing, membership, technology, statistics & records and investment research. CHX also offers free stock quotes. CHX may be researched online and CHX may be contacted online.

If we click onto "free stock quotes," the CHX website returns with stock. If we press "stock," a price data table appears, as does the sub search engine. You may also search CHX online by providing a search term for the sub search engine, Figure 5-4.

Contact
the **NYSE** @ *www.nyse.com*

Figure 5-5

The New York Stock Exchange traces its origins to a founding agreement in 1792. The NYSE was registered as a National Securities Exchange with the Securities and Exchange Commission on October 1, 1934. In 1971 the NYSE was incorporated as a non-profit corporation. The NYSE is committed to protecting, educating and supporting individual Investors.

As the world's premier Equities Market, the NYSE maintains an environment where the smallest or least sophisticated user of the marketplace is treated as fairly as a large institution.

A search of the trading floor reveals a sub-site called on the floor. On this sub-site you can see the floor of the NYSE with an explanation of the auction market and a NYSE trade. If you click "anatomy of a trade," you can see how a trade is made on the NYSE. Back to the NYSE home page and you can click "listed companies." A sub-search engine, listed companies, permits you to find an NYSE listed company, Figure 5-5.

Contact
the **PHLX** @ *www.phlx.com*

Figure 5-6

The Philadelphia Stock Exchange was formed in 1790 and is the first securities exchange in the United States. Currency options made the Philadelphia Exchange a round the clock operation. In September 1987, PHLX was the first securities exchange in the United States to introduce an evening trading session, chiefly to accommodate increasing demand for foreign currency options in the Far East.

In January 1989, PHLX responded to growing European demand by adding an early morning session. Although the hours were scaled back somewhat, trading occurs on the PHLX from 2:30 am to 2:30 pm, Philadelphia time.

In 1994 PHLX introduced the United Currency Options Market. UCOM, the first market in the world to offer customizable currency options in an Exchange environment, allows users to customize all aspects of a currency Option trade including: choice of exercise price, a selection of 110 currency Pairs, premium quotation as either units of currency or percent of underlying value, and customized expiration dates of up to two years.

PHLX offers products, a marketplace, news, publications, a calendar and educational material. PHLX also offers an online quote system through www.Quote.Com. The marketplace feature includes the most actively traded stocks, biggest gainers, biggest losers, volume alerts, points and figures, historical index data, option quote information, and information on currencies, a PHLX feature, Figure 5-6.

Contact
Contact **NASDAQ** @ *www.nasdaq.com*

Figure 5-7.

NASDAQ was founded in 1971. NASDAQ provides an environment for raising capital. As the market for NASDAQ's largest and most actively traded Securities, the NASDAQ National Market lists more than 4,400 securities. To be listed on the National Market, a company must satisfy stringent financial, capitalization, and corporate governance standards. NASDAQ National Market companies include some of the largest, best-known companies in the world.

NASDAQ's market for emerging growth companies, The NASDAQ Small Cap Market, lists nearly 1,800 individual securities. As the small capitalization tier of NASDAQ, the financial criteria for listing on this market are somewhat less stringent than on the NASDAQ National Market.

NASDAQ is not a floor-based exchange and no single specialist is used for trading, instead, a computer network is used to link buyers and sellers from around the world.

The NASDAQ website includes info quotes where you can obtain quotes for NASDAQ, AMEX & NYSE. Flash quotes are another feature on the NASDAQ website. You can also use it to search for company symbols. NASDAQ's website has a custom ticker. Figure 5-7.

> Contact
> the **OTCBB** @ *www.otcbb.com*

Figures 5-8

The OTC Bulletin Board began operation in 1990. OTCBB is a regulated quotation service that displays real-time quotes, last sale prices, and volume information in Over- The-Counter (OTC) Equity Securities. An OTC equity security generally is any equity that is not listed or traded on NASDAQ or a National Securities Exchange.

OTCBB Securities include national, regional, and foreign Equity Issues, Warrants, Units, American Depository Receipts, and Direct Participation Programs.

The OTCBB website has various options including market statistics, trading activity reports, Investor Information, a daily list, today's changes, general news, and newsletters, Figure 5-8.

Contact
the **BOTCC** @ *www.botcc.com*

Figure 5-9

FUTURES EXCHANGES

The Board of Trade Clearing Corporation is an independent corporation owned by clearing member firms which trade on the Chicago Board of Trade (CBOT) and the MidAmerica Commodity Exchange. In 1925, BOTCC became the first independent clearinghouse for Futures Markets in the United States. Figure 5-9.

BOTCC takes every submitted trade which is executed either in the trading pit or over an electronic trading system and continuously matches the clearing member buyer with the clearing member seller. Upon acceptance of a matched trade, the BOTCC acts as the buyer to every clearing member seller and the seller to every clearing member buyer. This way, BOTCC guarantees performance of all trades it accepts, in accordance with its bylaws, rules, policies and procedures. Since BOTCC's opening in 1925, no customer has lost money as a result of a default. Futures will be discussed in Chapter 15.

Contact
the **CBOT** @ *www.cbot.com*

Figure 5-10

Chicago Board of Trade was founded in 1865. CBOT provides a market for trading Futures and is called a Futures Exchange. CBOT is a not for profit membership association, Figure 5-10.

Contact
the **CME** @ *www.cme.com*

Figure 5-11

Chicago Mercantile Exchange is an international marketplace enabling institutions and businesses to manage their financial risks and allocate their assets. On its trading floors, buyers and sellers meet to trade Futures Contracts and options on Futures through the process of open outcry. In select contracts, trading continues virtually around the clock on the GLOBEX 2 electronic trading system.

The Merc's product line consists of Futures and Options on Futures within four general categories: agricultural commodities, foreign currencies, interest rates and stock indexes, Figure 5-11.

Contact
the **NYMEX** @ *www.nymex.com*

Figure 5-12

New York Mercantile Exchange is the world's largest physical Commodity Futures exchange. The New York Mercantile Exchange is a forum for trading energy and precious metals in North America. Figure 5-12.

Contact
the **NYBOT** @ *www.nybot.com*

Figure 5-13.

New York Board of Trade consists of the Coffee, Sugar, and Cocoa Exchanges along with The New York Cotton Exchange. Contracts currently traded on the CSCE include Futures and Options Contracts on world sugar, Arabian coffee, cocoa, cheddar cheese, nonfat dry milk, milk, butter, BFP milk and futures on domestic sugar and white sugar. The NYCE is the marketplace for Cotton Futures and Futures Options trading. Figure 5-13.

Chapter Six

WALL STREET
REGULATORS ON
THE INTERNET

Although **Wall Street regulation might be overlooked** by some, Wall Street Regulators, for example, the Securities and Exchange Commission, play a vital role in ensuring the vitality and soundness of the United States economy.

Contact
the **BPD** @ *www.publicdebt.treas.gov*

Figure 6-1

The Bureau of Public Debt regulates the sale of Treasury Securities and controls the raising of capital for the United States Government Treasury. Securities include treasury bills, notes and bonds. Treasury Securities are discussed in Chapter 13. Figure 6-1.

Contact
The **CFTC** @
www.cftc.gov

Figure 6-2

The Commodities & Futures Trading Commission was created by Congress in 1974 as an independent agency with the mandate to regulate Commodity Futures and Option Markets in the United States. The agency protects market participants against manipulation, abusive trade practices and fraud. Through effective oversight and regulation, the CFTC enables markets to better serve the nation's economy. The CFTC provides a mechanism for price discovery and a means of offsetting price risk. Figure 6-2.

The Commission is made up of five Commissioners appointed by the President under advisement and with consent of the Senate. Commissioners serve staggered five-year terms. The CFTC monitors markets and market participants closely by maintaining offices in cities that have futures exchanges: New York, Chicago, Kansas City and Minneapolis. For enforcement purposes, the Commission also maintains an office in Los Angeles.

The Commission has five major operating units: The Division of Economic Analysis, the Division of Trading and Markets, the Division of Enforcement, Office of the General Counsel and the Office of the Executive Director.

Contact
the **FRB** @ *www.bog.frb.fed.us*

Figure 6-3

The Federal Reserve Board On December 23, 1913, the Federal Reserve System, which serves as the Nation's Central Bank, was created by an Act of Congress. The System Is made up of a seven-member Board of Governors with headquarters in Washington, D.C. and twelve Reserve Banks located in major cities throughout the United States. Figure 6-3. The primary responsibility of the central bank is to influence the flow of money and credit in the nation's economy. The Federal Reserve Banks are involved with this function in several ways. First, five of the twelve Presidents of the Federal Reserve Banks serve along with the seven members of the Board of Governors, as members of the Open Market Committee (FOMC). The president of the Federal Reserve Bank of New York serves on a continuous basis. The other presidents serve one year terms on a rotating basis. The FOMC meets periodically in Washington, D.C. and determines policy with respect to purchases and sales of government securities in the open market. This action in turn affects the availability of money and credit in the economy.

The boards of directors of the Federal Reserve Banks initiate changes in the discount rate. The discount rate is the rate of interest on loans made by Reserve Banks to Depository Institutions at the discount window. Discount-rate changes must be approved by the Board of Governors.

Federal Reserve Banks also issue and redeem instruments of the public debt, such as Savings Bonds and Treasury Securities. The Federal Reserve has certain responsibilities for allotment and delivery of Government Securities and for wire transfer of Securities. In addition, the Reserve Banks make periodic payments of interest on outstanding obligations of the U.S. Treasury, Federal Agencies, and government-sponsored corporations.

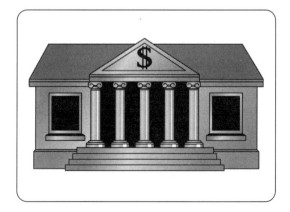

> Contact
> the **NASD** @ *www.nasd.com*

— *Figure 6-4* —

The National Association of Securities Dealers is the largest Securities Industry self regulatory organization in the United States. Through its subsidiaries, NASD Regulation Inc. and the NASDAQ, the NASD develops rules and regulations, conducts regulatory reviews of members' business activities, disciplines violators and designs, operates and regulates Securities markets. These services are provided for the benefit and protection of the Investor. Figure 6-4.

The NASD has a governing Board with a majority of outside Governors. The NASD and the Exchanges monitor trading, to make sure that customer Limit Orders are displayed and executed in keeping with the SEC and NASD rules. They also monitor prompt, real-time trade reporting and ensure that market makers honor their quotes. They do not allow fictitious trades or prices that are not being reported and make sure that markets are not dominated or controlled by any specific entity which could lead to arbitrary pricing. The NASD forbids "Securities parking". "Parking" is the holding or hiding of securities in someone else's name or a fictitious account.

The NASD watches to ensure that market makers maintain continuous markets. Underwriters must adhere to passive market-making rules that guarantee continuous liquidity. The NASD also disciplines stockbrokers and brokerage firms.

Contact
the **SEC** @ *www.sec.gov*

Figure 6-5

The Securities & Exchange Commission consists of five Presidential-appointed Commissioners, four divisions and 18 offices. With approximately 2,900 staff members, the SEC is small by federal agency standards. The SEC has headquarters in Washington, D.C. and has 11 regional and district offices throughout the United States. Figure 6-5.

The primary mission of the SEC is to protect investors and maintain the Integrity of the Securities Markets. Crucial to the SEC's effectiveness is its enforcement authority. Each year the SEC brings 400-500 civil enforcement actions against individuals and companies that break the Securities laws. Typical infractions include insider trading, accounting fraud, providing false or misleading information about securities and the companies that issue them. The SEC also oversees other key participants in the Securities world. They include stock exchanges, broker- dealers, investment advisors, mutual funds and public utility holding companies.

The Division of Enforcement was created in August 1972 to consolidate enforcement activities that previously had been handled by the various operating divisions at the SEC. The SEC's enforcement staff conduct investigations into possible violation of the federal securities laws, and prosecute the Commission's civil suits in the federal courts and administrative proceedings. The SEC may seek injunctions, prohibit future violations, obtain civil money penalties and the disgorgement of illegal profits, among other legal actions and remedies.

Chapter Seven

BROWSING
THE FINANCIAL
NEWS ONLINE

The Internet offers a wide variety of Internet financial news services which may be of interest to the investor or industry professional. Online financial news services are abundant and most provide free investment information. These services can be a valuable source of financial information without going to the news stand or picking up a newspaper.

Contact
ABC News.Com @ *www.abcnews.go.com*

Figure 7-1

ABC News.Com is a general news service with a business and financial section. In the business section you can search topics like: your business, your money, market details, the sectors, mutual funds and raw news. Click onto stock market details and articles on each subject will come up. Figure 7-1.

Contact
CNBC.com @ *www.cnbc.com*

Figure 7-2

CNBC.com provides stock market and financial news. CNBC has a quote box where you can enter a company name or symbol to obtain quotes, charts or boards. CNBC offers stories on stocks, markets and funds. Figure 7-2.

Contact
CNNfn.com @ *www.cnnfn.com*

Figure 7-3

CNNfn.com offers market news stories and sections on markets & investing, services, special reports & features. Click on markets & investing and you can find active charts and market news. You can also track your stock, check bonds and interest rates, examine world markets, currencies, tech stocks, most actives and stock quotes. Figure 7-3.

Contact **Money.Com** @ *www.money.com*

Figure 7-4

Money.Com features markets, news, investing, real estate, insurance, autos, retirement investment advice and tax suggestions. Money.Com also offers online quotes. Their markets section includes U.S. indices, and charts. Figure 7-4.

Contact **Reuters** @ *www.reuters.com*

Figure 7-5

Reuters is a general news website with a quotes section. Under quotes you will find world markets, U.S. markets and market news as well as key global indices, Figure, 7-5.

Contact
The Street.Com @ *www.thestreet.com*

Figure 7-6

The Street.Com offers a premium section and a free section. The premium section requires you to sign up. The free section does not. The free section has subjects such as markets, personal finance & investing basics. Figure 7-8.

Contact
USA Today Money @ *www.usatoday.com*

Figure 7-7

USA Today Money is a well developed financial website with a number of features including inside money, talks money, moneyline, small business, Wall Street summary, IPO's, economy track and daily money rates. USA Today Money also includes a marketplace section. Figure 7-7.

Contact
Wall Street Journal Interactive @ *www.public.wsj.com*

Figure 7-8

Wall Street Journal Interactive- The Wall Street Journal, a well known financial newspaper, has gone online. The Wall Street Journal Interactive also offers an interactive tour. Figure 7-8.

Chapter Eight

FINANCIAL WEBZINES

Webzines are online versions of magazines similar to the financial news publications we discussed in Chapter 7. The difference is that Webzine websites are structured more like magazines articles than newspaper articles and are intended to be read online like you would a magazine.

Contact
Barron's Online @ *www.interactive.wsj.com*

Figure 8-1

Barron's Online is a Webzine that is affiliated with the Wall Street Journal Interactive. For $59 you can have access to Baron's Online. This service includes weekday market commentary and analysis, markets statistics, interviews with mutual fund managers and analysis of specific stock situations to name just a few of the features of Barron's Online, Figure 8-1.

Contact
Business Week Online @ *www.businessweek.com*

Figure 8-2

Business Week Online is the online version of BusinessWeek magazine. The Webzine has a section devoted to the investor called the BW Investor. This section permits the person using the website to find articles on the following: stocks & markets, advice from S&P, the economy, mutual funds, investing basics and IPO's, Figure 8-2.

Contact
The Economist @ *www.economist.com*

Figure 8-3

The Economist provides a broad variety of stories ranging from politics to business, finance and economics. As with other Webzines, The Economist has stories that can be read online, Figure 8-3.

Contact
Forbes.com @ *www.forbes.com*

Figure 8-4

Forbes.com offers many of the features of Forbes Magazine, all online. Forbes is known for their lists and you can access some them online. For example you can download the Forbes 500 Annual Directory of America's Leading Companies, and the 500 Largest Private Companies in the U.S.. You can also search the Forbes 500 Annual Directory, Figure 8-4.

FORTUNE.COM

Contact
Fortune @ **www.fortuneinvestor.com**

Figure 8-5

Fortune features the Fortune Investor. You can access the Fortune 500 online by visiting the Fortune webzine site. Fortune also provides online company profiles of each of the Fortune 500 companies listed. Fortune has a number of other investment features to visit, online. Figure 8-5.

Contact
Kiplinger.com @ *www.kiplinger.com*

Figure 8-6

Kiplinger.com offers a Department called investments. Here you can choose stocks, funds or basics. In the stocks' section of the Website, you will find magazine articles on stocks. Figure 8-6.

Contact
Online Investor @ *www.investhelp.com*

Figure 8-7

The Online Investor has a number of investment related sub-sites including: a company spotlight, a guide to equity research, you & your broker, stock buy-backs, stock splits, splits performance among other features. This website is especially useful for stock research, Figure 8-7.

Chapter Nine

ONLINE
FINANCIAL
ANALYSIS

For the Investor who enjoys charts, this Chapter is for you. There are a number of online services that provide charts suitable for researching and monitoring investments. Charts are a good way to track stocks. We will discuss specific investments in later Chapters.

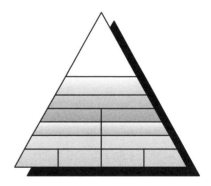

Contact
Ask Research @ *www.askresearch.com*

Figure 9-1

Ask Research is a free service for investors seeking daily charts, watch lists and other trading information. Ask Research has an online quote service. Select the NASDAQ Composite Index and a live 5-minute chart and indicators will appear on your screen, Figure 9-1.

Contact
Barchart.com @ *www.barchart.com*

Figure 9-2

Barchart.com is an online charting service that covers the commodity and stock markets. Stock market charts show market indices, market rates, volume leaders, price advances, and price declines. Barchart.com also displays commodity prices. This website has an interesting chart feature showing the net change of a currency on a specific date, Figure 9-2.

Contact
BigCharts @ *www.bigcharts.com*

Figure 9-3

BigCharts provides quotes, news, industries, markets, historical quotes and big reports. Click on index watch and BigCharts comes up with a chart tracking the Dow Jones Industrial average. There are also a number of other charts that may be of interest, Figure 9-3.

Contact
Daily Graphs Online @ *www.dailygraphs.com*

Figure 9-4

Daily Graphs Online is brought to you by Investor's Business Daily. Daily Graphs Online is subscription based. Daily Graphs Online offers a tour of Daily Graphs Online, Figure 9-4.

Contact
StockMaster.com @ *www.stockmaster.com*

Figure 9-5

StockMaster.com is a charting service that has quotes & research, top stocks, top funds, markets and other features. If we choose top stocks, StockMaster.com comes back with a listing of the top stock and their price changes. StockMaster charts each of the companies listed in Top Stocks, Figure 9-5.

Contact
StockTools @ *www.financialweb.com*

Figure 9-6

StockTools offer charts and real time quotes. If we search for options, StockMaster.com pulls up a sub-search engine that permits both stock and option quotes. StockTools features Index Options and most active options. StockTools also charts Index Options, Figure 9-6.

Chapter Ten

INTERNET FINANCIAL
RESEARCH
SERVICES

If **you are the type of Investor** or industry professional who likes to track stock, research companies, stock and other investments, then financial research websites will be of interest. A number of companies offer financial research services on the World Wide Web, for free. Others charge a relatively small fee for monthly access to research data bases. If you invest routinely and conduct your own research, the fees may be nominal as compared to the benefit you will derive from these financial research services.

BRIEFING.COM®

Live Market Analysis

Contact
Briefing.Com @ *www.briefing.com*

Figure 10-1

Briefing.Com, a financial research service, offers market comments, quotes and charts, portfolios, sector ratings and other services free of charge. For $9.95 per month you can log into Briefing.Com's live stock analysis. For $25.00 per month you can have premium service, Figure 10-1.

Contact
Companies Online @ *www.companiesonline.com*

Figure 10-2

Companies Online allows you to research information on companies of interest. You may browse by industry or you may search by criteria, Figure 10-2.

Contact
Dun & Bradstreet *@ www.dnbcorp.com*

Figure 10-3

Dun & Bradstreet is well known for its financial research. Dun & Bradstreet Corporation is the owner of Dun & Bradstreet and Moody's Investors Service. They draw from a global database of more than 50 million businesses. The Dun & Bradstreet Million Dollar Database provides information on 1,260,000 U.S. businesses including stock quotes and SEC filings, Figure 10-3 .

Contact
FinanceWise *@ www.financewise.com*

Figure 10-4

FinanceWise allows you to research companies. You can also search for topics such as capital markets and investments, Figure 10-4.

Contact
First Call @ *www.firstcall.com*

Figure 10-5

First Call Corporation (a Thomson Financial company) provides a global research network of real-time commingled equity and fixed income research, corporate news, quantitative and shareholdings' data. Although this website is primarily for the industry professional, it may be worth your time, Figure 10-5.

Contact
Market Guide Investor @ *www.marketguide.com*

Figure 10-6

Market Guide Investor has a database of more than 12,000 publicly traded companies. Market Guide Investor also offers real time quotes, Figure 10-6.

Contact
MoneyCentral @ *www.moneycentral.msn.com*

Figure 10-7

MSN MoneyCentral (MSN Microsoft) offers MoneyCentral. MoneyCentral permits you to track investments, research markets, conduct stock and mutual fund research, find stock and contact brokers. To conduct research, MoneyCentral has a download feature for MSN MoneyCentral version 7.0 Software, Figure 10-7.

Contact
Reuters moneynet @ *www.moneynet.com*

Figure 10-8

Reuters moneynet website includes a portfolio, quotes, news, charts, markets and research. Moneynet's research section allows you to research stock according to stock classifications listed on the search tool bar. Once you conduct a search, moneynet provides a list of stock meeting the search criteria. You can then research a particular stock, Figure 10-8.

Contact
Zacks
@ *www.zacks.com*

Figure 10-9

Zacks Investment Research is a full service quantitative research firm offering products including data feeds to equity models, software and Internet applications. One interesting feature on Zacks site, is the free personal portfolio tracker and stock screener which allow you to create multiple portfolios with multiple views to track stocks that you own or are tracking. Zacks is definitely worthwhile, Figure 10-9.

Contact
Business Wire @ *www.businesswire.com*

Figure 10-10

Business Wire is a news wire service that delivers news from more sources than any other business news wire service in the world. It has content from more than 40,000 organizations including Fortune 1000 and NASDAQ companies. It is an independent commercial news wire that is a solid source of direct business news information, Figure 10-10.

Contact
MoneyCentral Investor @ *news.moneycentral.msn.com*

Figure 10-11

MoneyCentral Investor offers sections on Portfolio, Markets, Stocks, Funds as well as a section devoted to Investors. The Market Report segment of the site provides a stock ticker from Briefing.com with sector watches showing both strong and weak industries. This industry specific feature is particularly useful when conducting industry research for stock purchases, Figure 10-11.

Contact
Quicken @ *www.quicken.com*

Figure 10-12

Quicken.com is a good source of financial information from the company that brings Quicken Software. Quicken has a number good financial sections that are worth exploration including a portfolio device that is interactive and other financial planning features, Figure 10-12.

Contact
Renaissance IPO @ *www.ipo-fund.com*

Figure 10-13

Renaissance IPO is one of the few websites on the Internet that deals exclusively with IPO's (Initial Public Offerings of Stock). It has features which include IPO News, IPO Commentary; IPO of the Week and IPO Calendars. If you are interested in IPO's then visit Renaissance and see what they have to offer, Figure 10-13.

Contact
Standard & Poors @ *www.standardpoor.com*

Figure 10-14

Standard & Poors, a premier financial service, provides Capital Markets Services, including CUSIP and the Blue List; Fund Services (Managed Funds Ratings); Investment Services and Rating Services for corporates, derivatives, financial institutions and insurance among other services. Research is the primary feature for this well known company, Figure 10-14.

Contact
Yahoo Finance @ *www.quote.yahoo.com*

Figure 10-15

Yahoo Finance has a number of categories the Investor can search under to find valuable investment information. This includes: Markets, News, Mutual Funds, International, Research & Education, Personal Finance and other features. Yahoo Finance is a sub-component of the Yahoo search engine and is particularly useful as it groups a number of finance related websites which can be easily visited. It is one of the few investing sites with an international investment section.

You can find Market Overview, Most Actives, IPO's, Earnings, Indices, Splits, Options, Top Performing Mutual Funds and many other valuable features here, Figure 10-15.

Chapter Eleven

CYBER-STOCK

The following Chapters focus on an explanation of investments with online illustrations. Chapter 11 focuses on stocks. Stock represents an equity ownership in a corporation. The term equity ownership is used to distinguish stock from bonds. A stockholder actually owns a percentage of the corporation issuing the stock. The larger the corporation,

generally, the less the ownership interest. A bondholder is a creditor to the corporation since the bondholder, by virtue of the bond, has lent money to the corporation. A corporate creditor has no ownership interest. Instead, a bondholder has certain rights of priority upon liquidation of the corporation, should it have to file for bankruptcy protection under Federal Law. Bonds will be discussed in Chapter 13.

A corporation issues stock to raise capital for the company. Although capital can be raised by a bond sale, a corporation may prefer to raise capital by stock sale in exchange for a reduction in the percentage of corporate ownership. A Stock issuance may be more desirable than an early accumulation of debt by a new company. The initial stock sale is known as the initial public offering or IPO. Once the stock is sold, it may be traded actively on one of the nation's stock markets.

Corporations can be both publicly and privately held. A privately held corporation issues stock, however, it is a private company and will not be listed on a stock exchange such as the New York Stock Exchange. Public corporations, like IBM, are owned by the investing public.

In a nutshell, stock represents ownership in a corporation. Stock can increase or decrease in value depending upon how well a corporation or industry in general performs. Stock is generally divided into common and preferred stock. Common Stock is the simplest form of corporate ownership by the investing public. Figure 11-1 Preferred Stock often costs more than common stock but it may not have the same privileges as common stock. The trade off for owners of preferred stock is that it has priority over common stock in the event the corporation goes bankrupt. Preferred stock can be cumulative or convertible. The use of these terms merely provides the legal distinctions between the two. For example, the owner of purely non-cumulative preferred stock will not be receive back pay if a corporation misses a dividend, whereas, the owner of cumulative preferred stock will receive a late payment. Convertible preferred stock merely allows the owner of the stock to convert from preferred to common stock.   We will now turn to investment related websites. Caveat emptor (Buyer Beware) is always applicable especially when choosing investments, so

Common Stock Data

The tables below present the quarterly high and low closing sales prices and dividend information for the Company's stock as furnished by The Nasdaq Stock Market's National Market. There were 1,686 holders of record of the company's common stock as of December 31, 1995.

1995

Quarter	High	Low	Dividends Declared Per Share
First	$43.75	$33.50	$.04
Second	$54.50	$40.50	$.04
Third	$64.00	$52.81	$.04
Fourth	$85.75	$62.25	$.04
		Total	**$.16**

1994

Quarter	High	Low	Dividends Declared Per Share
First	$26.38	$20.88	$.04
Second	$31.13	$20.75	$.04
Third	$34.50	$24.50	$.04
Fourth	$36.13	$29.00	$.04
		Total	**$.16**

Figure 11-1

be selective. A note of caution about using stock message boards as a source for stock tips. Message boards have been used in market manipulation scams and many unwary investors have been hurt. It is illegal to manipulate stock prices. Be careful. Now let's focus on stock specific websites and delve into cyber-stock.

Contact
BigPlayStocks @ *www.bigplaystocks.com*

Figure 11-2

BigPlayStocks.com is a subscription based Internet stock website. BigPlayStocks charges $19.95 to $89.95 per month depending on the features you select. You can participate in the live trading room and see BigPlayStocks stock jock trade in real time. You can trade right along with them, Figure 11-2.

Contact
Great Picks.Com @ *www.great-picks.com*

Figure 11-3

Great Picks.Com is a subscription-based stock profiling company. Great Picks.Com profiles stock and lists their record of prior stock picks on the website. Figure 11-3.

Contact
Just Quotes.Com @ *www.justquotes.com*

Figure 11-4

Just Quotes.Com provides a number of articles on investing. If you search the word "trading", Just Quotes.Com turns up a list of trading articles. If you would like more information on trading in general or other financial topics, Just Quotes.Com is a good source, Figure 11-4.

Contact
Stocksmart.Com @ *www.stocksmart.com*

Figure 11-5

Stocksmart.Com is also a subscription-based service. For $12.95 you can receive profiles of companies, research reports on 20,000 companies, review industry and sector news as well as other features. You can also take a site tour of the Stocksmart.Com website, Figure 11-5.

Contact
Stockselector.com @ *www.stockselector.com*

Figure 11-6

Stockselector.com is a registration-based stock selection service. Stockselector has a fair amount of information on stocks with updates on events such as stock splits and mergers. Figure 11-6.

Contact
Quotes.com @ *www.quotes.com*

Figure 11-7.

Quotes.com is the source for quotes. It offers Stock Quotes, Consumer Goods Quotes, Insurance Quotes, Real Time Quotes, and Delayed Quotes. Quotes.com is often used by industry professionals because of their Real Time Quotes feature. If you need quotes then Quotes.com is a good starting point, Figure 11-7.

Chapter Twelve

HIGH TECH
STOCK

Stock is a broad term and has numerous sub-categories depending on the type of industry. The technology sector is one of those sub-components and since this book is geared toward using information technology to increase investment knowledge and skill, high tech stocks and websites related to technology merit discussion.

Contact
CPMnet @ *www.cmpnet.com*

Figure 12-1

CPMnet is a solid source of information on Technology. If you wish to become a proficient trader of High Techstocks, it might be wise to get to know the Technology Industry first. CPMnet is a well-developed website which will permit the investor to access a fair amount of information on the Technology and the High Tech Industry. CPMnet is a great starting point for someone interested in learning how to invest here, Figure 12-1.

Contact
Good Morning Silicon Valley @ *www.mercurycenter.com*

Figure 12-2

Good Morning Silicon Valley is a website very specific to Silicon Valley High Tech. SiliconValley.com has Silicon Valley news, columns on the High Tech Industry, and a company watch section. The High Tech Company watch features lists of High Tech companies and provides related stories. This is the main feature of the website, Figure 12-2.

Contact
Silicon Investor @ *www.siliconinvestor.com*

Figure 12-3

The Silicon Investor is designed for investors of Silicon Valley Stock. The Silicon Investor has technical charts, a stock screener and a site map, Figure 12-3.

Contact
Sofcom @ *www.sofcom.com*

Figure 12-4

Sofcom is a general website with business features that include investment advice and high tech stock prices. It is a good website to review if you want to know the latest price on High Tech Stocks. An added benefit of the Silicon Investor is that it has direct links to specific High Tech companies, Figure 12-4.

Contact
TechStockInvestor @
www.techstockinvestor.com

Figure 12-5

TechStockInvestor is subscription based. For $39 you can sign up for the Top 50 Stock Listings. TechStockInvestor also has the Top 10 Monthly Listing. If you select Yahoo, TechStockInvestor brings up a company profile of Yahoo. There are a number of other features worth examining. If you are into Technology Stock, the subscription fee may be well worth it, Figure 12-5.

Chapter Thirteen

BONDS ONLINE

Bonds can be viewed as the opposite of stock. A stockholder owns a small part of a corporation. A bondholder lends money to a corporation or government. Bonds fall into three main categories: government, municipal and corporate. Corporate bonds are issued by corporations, municipal bonds are issued by a state or municipality and Government bonds are issued by the United States government.

GOVERNMENT BONDS

Government bonds fall into three categories: savings bonds, treasury bills, notes & bonds, and STRIPS. All of these are offered by the Bureau of Public Debt.

Savings Bonds

U.S. Savings Bonds are currently classified into two main categories, Series EE/E, and Series HH/H.

Series EE/E savings bonds are accrual securities. Interest is periodically added to the amount you originally paid to establish their current redemption value. As you receive this redemption value, it represents the return of your original investment plus the interest that you have earned while you held the bond.

Series HH/H are current income securities. The redemption value of the Bonds remain constant at exactly the amount you invested and your interest is paid to you every six months. When you cash an H/HH Bond, you receive your original investment back. Savings Bonds can be purchased Online.

Treasury Bills fall into three categories: Thirteen weeks, Twenty-six weeks, and Fifty- two weeks. Thirteen-weeks and twenty-six week Bills are offered each week. Fifty-two week Bills are offered every four weeks.

Treasury Notes & Bonds are arranged in three categories: 2-year Notes, 5-year Notes, 10- year Notes, and thirty-year Bonds. Two-year Notes are issued once a month. 5-year and 10-year Notes are auctioned in May, August and November. Thirty-year Bonds are auctioned in February and August.

Treasury STRIPS were introduced in February 1985. STRIPS is the acronym for Separate Trading of Registered Interest and Principal of Securities. The STRIPS program lets investors hold and trade the individual interest and principal components of eligible Treasury Notes and Bonds as a separate Security. When a treasury fixed-principal or inflation-indexed note or bond is stripped, each interest payment and the principal payment becomes a separate zero-coupon security. Zero Coupon Securities are discussed toward the end of this Chapter.

Each component of a STRIP has its own identifying number, and can be held or traded separately. For example, a Treasury Note with 10 years remaining to maturity consists of a single principal payment at maturity and 20 interest payments, one every six months for 10 years. When this is converted to STRIPS, each of the twenty interest payments and the principal payment becomes a separate Security. STRIPS are also called zero-coupon securities because the only time an investor receives a payment during the life of a STRIP is when it matures. STRIPS cannot be purchased directly from the Treasury. Instead, you must go through a brokerage firm or a bank that sells STRIPS.

Municipal Bonds are issued by the state or municipality to raise money for a particular purpose. Municipal bonds come in the following forms: general obligation bonds, industrial development bonds, moral obligation bonds, and revenue bonds. Municipal bonds can be purchased from brokerage firms who sell municipals or online through a company such as MUNI Direct (www.munidirect.com).

General Obligation Bonds are issued through public entities to assist in private development of activities. These bonds can either be tax-exempt revenue bonds, not guaranteed by the governmental unit or general obligation bonds which may be taxable or tax exempt. These bonds are backed by the general faith and credit of the issuing entity to assure repayment of the bonds.

Industrial Development Revenue Bonds finance fixed assets or facilities which are then used by a corporation. The corporation is in turn responsible for repaying the IDRB's and the Bonds are backed by the general credit of the corporation.

Moral Obligation Bonds impose no legal obligation upon the issuing authority for repayment of the bond. The obligation to repay the bondholder is purely a moral one on the part of the municipality.

GOVERNMENT AGENCY SECURITIES

Government Agency Securities are issued by entities which are affiliated with the United States Government either directly or through a Congressional Charter, for example, Ginnie Mae.

Contact
Fannie Mae @ *www.fanniemae.com*

Figure 13-1

Fannie Mae was created by Congress in 1938 to bolster the housing industry during the Depression. Fannie Mae is a private, shareholder-owned company that works to make sure mortgage money is available. Fannie Mae does not lend money directly. Instead, Fannie Mae operates under a Congressional charter that directs it to channel efforts into increasing the availability and affordability of home ownership for low, moderate and middle-income Americans. Fannie Mae receives no Government funds and is actively traded on the NYSE, and other exchanges (FNM), Figure 13-1.

Fannie Mae is one of the world's largest issuers of debt securities. Fannie Mae Debt Securities trade in the U.S. agency market. Fannie Mae auctions these Debt Securities and sells Mortgaged-Backed Securities.

Contact
Freddie Mac @ *www.freddiemac.com*

Figure 13-2

Freddie Mac is also a stockholder-owned corporation chartered by Congress in 1970 to create a continuous flow of funds to mortgage lenders, in support of home ownership, and rental housing. Freddie Mac purchases mortgages from lenders and packages them into securities that are sold to investors. By doing so, Freddie Mac ultimately provides homeowners and renters with lower housing costs and better access to home financing. Freddie Mac sells both Debt Securities and Mortgage Securities. Mortgage Securities are sold through the Securities Sales and Trading Group, Freddie Mac's mortgage securities dealer operation, Figure 13-2.

Contact

Ginnie Mae @ *www.ginniemae.gov*

Figure 13-3

Ginnie Mae works under the Department of Housing and Urban Development (HUD). As with Fannie Mae and Freddie Mac, Ginnie Mae operates a Mortgage Back Securities program. Ginnie Mae Mortgage Backed Securities are guaranteed and backed by the full faith and credit of the United States. This means that if the issuer fails to make payment, Ginnie Mae will make the payment to the investor, Figure 13-3.

Contact

Sallie Mae @ *www.salliemae.com*

Figure 13-4

Sallie Mae provides funds for student and parent loans by purchasing education loans from lenders. Sallie Mae provides services to help colleges deliver loans to their students more effectively and efficiently. Sallie Mae sells student loan packages on the Secondary Market. The stock of Sallie Mae's parent company, SLM Holding Corporation, is publicly traded on the NYSE (SLM), Figure 13-4.

CORPORATE BONDS

There are different types of Corporate Bonds and it is beneficial to understand each type for investment purposes. Many of the brokerage firms sell bonds online. We will discuss brokerage firms in Chapter 16. I will compile a simple list of Corporate Bond types.

Bearer Bonds are issued without registration of the Bondholder on the books of the issuing corporation.

Callable Bonds have a call price attached. This means that the corporation that has issued the bond has maintained the legal right to purchase the Bond at a set price, the call price, prior to the maturity of the bond.

Collateral Trust Bonds exist when the issuing corporation deposits securities as collateral equal to the value of the bond to support the issue.

Convertible Bonds are issued to permit the Bondholder to convert the Bond to a set number of common stock at a prearranged price.

Debentures are bonds which are collateralized by the general credit of the issuing corporation.

Subordinated Debentures are unsecured Bonds with a subordinated claim to the corporation's assets upon Bankruptcy and liquidation.

Zero Coupon Bonds are a corporate form of STRIPS discussed previously. A Zero is a Bond purchased at a discount from the face value of the Bond. Upon maturity, the full face value is paid to the Bondholder.

Chapter Fourteen

MUTUAL FUNDS, CDs & ANNUITIES ON THE WEB

As with stocks and bonds, brokerage firms offer mutual funds. CD's are typically offered by banks, and annuities are offered by insurance companies. What follows is a discussion of specific websites that are directly related to mutual funds, CDs & annuities.

MUTUAL FUNDS are investments that pool money from many people and invest in a portfolio of stocks, bonds and securities. A mutual fund offers investors the advantages of diversification and professional management.

Contact
American Express Financial Advisors @
www.americanexpress.com

Figure 14-1

American Express Financial Advisors is a brokerage firm that offers mutual funds, annuities, certificates, insurance, IRA's, lending products, and deposit products. American Express Financial Advisors offer personal trust services. You can request the prospectus for each of the products online. It also offers investment services, personal financial services, business and workplace services, Figure 14-1.

ARIEL MUTUAL FUNDS

Contact
Ariel Mutual funds.Com @ *www.arielmutualfunds.com*

Figure 14-2

Ariel Mutual funds.Com sells three types of mutual funds: The Ariel fund, Ariel appreciation fund and the Ariel premier bond fund. Ariel provides online services including exchanges between Ariel mutual funds and other online services. You can also research the performance of the Ariel mutual funds online and receive a prospectus, Figure 14-2.

Contact
Bloomberg.com @ *www.bloomberg.com*

Figure 14-3

Bloomberg.com provides a website featuring the top U.S. mutual funds: the year to date. Bloomberg also provides a list of the top 25 U.S. funds. When using the Top 25 section of the website, you can find a profile of mutual funds, Figure 14-3.

Contact
Findafund.com @ *www.findafund.com*

Figure 14-4

Findafund.com is an online mutual fund service that allows you to research mutual funds by name, category or by ticker. You can research a particular fund and find out specific information on that fund's performance record, Figure 14-4.

MutualFundsnet.com

Contact
Mutual fundsnet.Com @ *www.mutualfundsnet.com*

Figure 14-5.

Mutual funds Online is the online version of the Institute for Econometric Research. Econometric publishes the Webzine, Mutual fund Magazine.Com, and print magazines: Mutual funds Magazine, and Mutual fund Forecaster, among other publications. The Mutual funds Online website has a number of features including a chat room, fund of the day, dog of the day and new 5-star funds, Figure 14-5.

Contact
S&P Personal Wealth @ www.personalwealth.com

Figure 14-6

S&P Personal Wealth offers information on mutual funds, among other features. You can find daily fund news, fund screens, S&P select funds, fund insights, fund strategies, fund spotlight, and other features including a daily scorecard of the best & worst performers, Figure 14-6.

Contact
Yahoo! Finance @ *www.biz.yahoo.com*

Figure 14-7

Yahoo! Finance has a section devoted to mutual fund top performers. The funds are divided into categories of U.S. stock funds, bond funds, international stock funds, and hybrid funds. You can search for overall top performers or search by fund type, Figure 14-7.

CDs

CDs are certificates of deposit. A CD is a money market instrument issued by a bank or a company that has a set interest rate and maturity date. CDs may be issued for as low as $100. CDs that are in denominations of $100,000 or more are called jumbo CDs. Maturities can range from a few weeks to several years. CD's are often sold by banks. Since CDs are quite common to local banks, the following website should provide a sufficient illustration.

Contact
Los Alamos National Bank @ *www.lanb.com*

Figure 14-8

Los Alamos National Bank offers Certificates of Deposits. Terms for Los Alamos National Bank CDs are for 90 days to 60 months. The interest rate increases depending upon the term. The longer the term the higher the rate, Figure 14-8.

ANNUITIES

Annuities consist of a financial contract between the purchaser and the seller, often an insurance company. The Annuitant (person purchasing the annuity) places money in the annuity, and in exchange, the company agrees to pay income in the future.

During the accumulation period, money is placed into the annuity in a series of contributions or in one lump sum. That money grows, tax-deferred, at a certain rate. During the payout period the Annuitant receives the money placed in the annuity, along with earnings on the annuity. Most annuity contracts also have several payout options such as payments for as long as you live, or a lump sum. An annuity may be deferred or immediate. Immediate annuities pay within a very short period of depositing funds for the annuity. Deferred annuities require the Annuitant to wait until a specific date for payment.

Annuities can be variable or fixed. Variable annuities encompass investments within the annuity which are variable, for example a stock. A fixed annuity would invest in a bond or other fixed rate investment.

Contact
4Annuities.Com @ *www.4annuities.com*

Figure 14-9

4Annuities.Com lists annuity providers and services. 4Annuities.com also has an information & resources guide to annuities that may serve useful, Figure 14-9.

Contact
Annuities Online @ *www.annuitiesonline.com*

Figure 14-10

Annuities Online provides information on annuities. Annuities Online includes a section featuring annuities sold by particular companies with statistics on each type of Annuity sold, Figure 14-10.

Contact
GE Financial Network @ *www.getn.com*

Figure 14-11.

GE Financial Network offers both immediate and deferred annuities. Deferred annuities are offered in fixed, variable and indexed form, Figure 14-11.

Contact
TIAA-CREF *@ www.tiaa-cref.org*

Figure 14-12

TIAA-CREF offers personal annuities, both variable and fixed. TIAA-CREF has designed their annuities for Teachers, Figure 14-12.

Contact
QuickQuote.com *@ www.quickquote.com*

Figure 4-13

QuickQuote.com offers annuities online. You can receive a quote on an annuity through the QuikQuote system, Figure 4-13.

Chapter Fifteen

OPTIONS, FUTURES &
COMMODITIES
ON THE INTERNET

O**PTIONS** consist of the right, but not the obligation, to buy or sell a particular item at a certain price for a limited time. Only the seller of the option is obligated to perform. A call consists of an option to buy a Commodity, Security or Futures contract at a specified price anytime between the time sale and the expiration date of the options contracts. A Put is an option to

sell a Commodity, Security, or Futures contract at a specified price at any time between date of sale and the expiration of the options contract. The option premium is the price the seller receives for the rights granted by the option.

FUTURES & COMMODITIES

Futures & Commodities consists of a futures contract, which is an agreement to purchase or sell a commodity for delivery in the future: (1) at a price that is determined at initiation of the contract; (2) which obligates each party to the contract to fulfill the contract at the specified price; (3) which is used to assume or shift price risk; and (4) which may be satisfied by delivery or offset.

A Commodity consists of specifically enumerated Agricultural Commodity all other goods and articles, except onions, and all services, rights, and interests in which contracts for future delivery are presently or in the future may be dealt.

A Commodity Option is a unilateral contract which gives the buyer the right to buy or sell a specified quantity of a Commodity at a specific price within a specified period of time, regardless of the market price of that Commodity. Websites related to options, commodities & futures, follow.

Contact
Bloomberg.com @ *www.bloomberg.com*

Figure 15-1

Bloomberg.com was discussed in Chapter 14. Bloomberg has a commodities section which could be explored, Figure 15-1.

Contact
ino.com @
www.ino.com

Figure 15-2

ino.com is affiliated with QuoteWatch.com and is subscription based. ino.com offers charts & quotes on futures. ino.com also allows you to search for Options and it provides charts, Figure 15-2.

Contact
OptionInvestor.com @ *www.optioninvestor.com*

Figure 15-3

OptionInvestor.com is a subscriber based Options Advisory Service. OptionInvestor.Com was introduced in 1997. For $39.95 per month, OptionInvestor.com delivers option strategies and trading opportunities. The subscription service includes: market commentary, market analysis, market posture, Option strategies, trade recommendations, and trader tools, Figure 15-3.

Contact
OptionsSource.com @ *www.optionsource.com*

Figure 15-4

OptionsSource.com is an Options related website that is provided as a service by Schaeffer's Investment Research publisher of Option Advisor. OptionsSource.com offers tools such as quotes & charts, analysis, including commentaries and education, Figure 15-4.

Contact
Stricknet.Com @ *www.stricknet.com*

Figure 15-5

Stricknet.Com is a subscription-based options' service. For $35 per month Stricknet.Com offers option picks, daily commentary, covered calls, and a naked put list among other services, Figure 15-5.

Contact
Strikeprice.Com @ *www.financialweb.com*

Figure 15-6

Strikeprice.Com is a subscription-based service that includes real-time quotes and an option watcher service, among other features, Figure 15-6.

Chapter Sixteen

ONLINE BROKERAGE
FIRMS & TRADING
SERVICES

O nline **trading services** fall into two categories: Brokerage firms providing online trading or investing, and trading services where you trade alone, for a discounted trading fee. I attempt to provide a balance between full service brokerage firms and discount trading services.

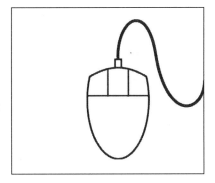

Contact
American Express Online Brokerage @ *www.americanexpress.com*

Figure 16-1

American Express Online Brokerage is a component of American Express Company. American Express Company is a global travel, financial and Network Service Provider. Founded in 1850, the Company serves individuals with charge and credit cards, traveler checks, and other stored value products. It also offers financial planning, brokerage services, mutual funds, insurance and other investment products.

American Express Online Brokerage provides online trading in both stocks and mutual funds. American Express' online trading service is illustrated in Chapter 17. Figure 16-1.

Contact
Citicorp Investment Services @ *www.citibank.com*

Figure 16-2

Citicorp Investment Services offer online trading through Citicorp Investment Services and Citibank Direct Access PC banking accounts. Provided you have an account with Citicorp Investment Services, City Bank and Citicard, and Citibank Direct Access, you can place orders to buy and sell stocks, bonds, mutual funds and other securities for as low as $19.95 a trade, Figure, 16-2.

Contact
E*Trade @ *www.etrade.com*

Figure 16-3

E*Trade started as E*TRADE Securities, Inc., in 1992 as an all electronic brokerage, offering online investing services through America Online and CompuServe. In 1996 www.etrade.com was launched. E*Trade charges different rates depending upon the type of investment traded and the number of trades. For example, the first 29 trades of listed stocks, costs $14.95 with a rebate for trades in excess of 29, Figure 16-3.

Contact
Fidelity Investments @ *www.300.fidelity.com*

Figure 16-4

Fidelity Investments offers a range of Fidelity and non-Fidelity mutual funds, and discount brokerage services directly to individual investors. The Brokerage Group comprises five brokerage service businesses. Fidelity offers online trading with commissions as low as $14.95, Figure 16-4.

Contact
Morgan Stanley Dean Witter @ *www.online.msdw.com*

Figure 16-5

Morgan Stanley Dean Witter Online provides investment services and information via the Internet. They began doing so in August of 1995. Morgan Stanley Dean Witter's online trading services are discussed in Chapter 17. Figure 16-5.

Contact
Mr. Stock @ *www.secure.mrstock.com*

Figure 16-6

Mr. Stock was founded in 1993. In 1997 Mr. Stock began its transformation to online brokerage specializing in options-execution. Mr. Stock charges various fees depending upon the investment traded. For example, a stock trade with market orders of greater than 5,000 shares costs $14.95, plus an excess share charge, Figure 16-6.

Contact
Quick & Reilly @ *www.quick-reilly.com*

Figure 16-7

Quick & Reilly a member of the NYSE, offers online trading of a number of products including stocks, options, bonds and mutual funds. Online commissions are $14.95 for market orders, and $19.95 for limit orders up to 5,000 shares, Figure 16-7.

Contact
ScoTTrade @ *www.scottrade.com*

Figure 16-8

ScotTrade an online trading service, offers Internet trades for Nasdaq and listed stock for as low as $7. Other trade prices vary depending upon the type of trade, Figure 16-8.

130

Contact
Ameritrade @
www.ameritrade.com

Figure 16-9.

    Ameritrade offers $8 Internet trades. Ameritrade provides convenient account access and a secure online trading experience. Whether you trade 100 shares or 10,000 shares, Internet equity market orders are still $8. Ameritrade also lowered their commissions on Internet options market trades to $8 plus $1.75 per contract. Equity and options stop and limit orders are $5 more, Figure 16-9.

Contact
Brown & Company @ *www.brownco.com*

Figure 16-10

Brown & Company offers market orders of $5. They are a deep discount broker for those experienced investors who make their own investment decisions and are willing to manage their own accounts. They appeal to the savvy investor, Figure 16-10.

Contact
Charles Schwab @ *www.schwab.com*

— *Figure 16-11.* —————————————

Charles Schwab offers a number of Accounts, Investments, Mutual Funds, Quotes and Research Services to the investor. They also offer Investment Basics, Planning Tools and a Glossary. Schwab is the world's largest online broker, Figure 16-11.

Contact
Datek Online @ *www.datek.com*

— *Figure 16-12.* —————————————

Datek Online is a trading brokerage firm that offers commissions of $9.99 for online equity trades up to 5000 shares on all order types for stocks listed on the NYSE, AMEX and NASDAQ.

Datek offers Equities, Mutual Funds, IRA's Real Time Quotes and other online brokerage services, Figure 16-12.

Contact
CSFBdirect *@ www.csfbdirect.com*

Figure 16-13

DLJ Direct is now CSFBdirect. CSFBdirect offers a diversified range of investment products and services to sophisticated, self-directed Investors. Limit orders and other types of trades including online investing cost $20, Figure 16-13.

Contact
National Discount Brokers *@*
www.ndb.com

National Discount Brokers | ndb.com

Figure 16-14

National Discount Brokers has an online application which permits' investors to commence trading in as little as 48 hours. You can also request a new account kit which is sent via US Mail. You may also visit their Retirement Center for IRA accounts, Figure16-14.

Contact
TD Waterhouse @ *www.tdwaterhouse.com*

Figure16-15

TD Waterhouse is the world's second largest online discount brokerage firm only behind Charles Schwab. TD Waterhouse is primarily oriented toward online trading. However, it also services clients by providing a host of investments including Mutual Funds, Stock, Bonds, Annuities. Trading consists of Stock, Bonds, Mutual Funds, Options and Commodities.

TD Waterhouse offers low commission rates of a $12 flat fee on equity market orders, up to 5000 shares when orders are placed online. For more information check out TD Waterhouse's commission schedule at their website, Figure 16-15

Chapter Seventeen

TRADING
& INVESTING
ONLINE

By now you should be hooked up to the Internet and have surfed through a large number of financial websites. You have traveled through Wall Street via the World Wide Web to understand 21st Century Wall Street. To learn how Wall Street works you have browsed the financial news and financial webzines. You know how to conduct financial analysis and research online, and you are familiar with cyber-stock, high tech stock, bonds, mutual funds, CDs, annuities, options, futures & commodities. You have the tools to make your own choice; continue to invest with a brokerage firm, the traditional way, or invest online.

ONLINE TRADING & INVESTING

You are at the forefront of the online investing revolution and have the power to use the knowledge you have acquired to trade and invest online. Now that you have tapped the power of the Internet, you are well prepared to trade online.

Online trading is a term that narrowly describes what a small number of investors and discount brokers began a few years ago, that is, trading stock on the Internet. What if you purchased a mutual fund or an annuity online? Would that still be an online trade? Purchasing an annuity does not constitute trading. It is generally a long-term investment; not typically traded on the secondary market. The term online trading has become passe because it is too narrow. We are at the forefront of what I term "Online Investing."

Online investing is a broader term that encompasses online trading, and making investment purchases such as mutual funds, bonds, annuities, and a

host of other products that are available online. In either case, we will discuss three examples of online investing services; American Express' Online Brokerage, Morgan Stanley Dean Witter's online trading service, and Wall St. Access' trading service.

Contact

American Express Online Brokerage @ *www.americanexpress.com*

Figures 17-1

AMERICAN EXPRESS ONLINE BROKERAGE TOUR

American Express offers a number of features to their online investing service: real-time customized stock quotes, stock orders, and mutual fund access. The American Express tour is helpful to understand online investing & trading in that it permits the investor to see how an online trading account is established, and how the process works.

The American Express Tour fully explains what an investor is to expect when trading online with a Brokerage firm. It begins with an explanation of how to establish an e-mail account with American Express. You then learn how to check your account balances, manage your portfolio, place stock orders, view major indexes, choose mutual funds, chart your progress, and even pay your bills online.

Contact
Morgan Stanley Dean Witter Online @ *www.online.msdw.com*

Figure 17-2

MORGAN STANLEY DEAN WITTER ONLINE

Morgan Stanley Dean Witter's online service is very specific as to how to actually trade stock online. The demo-account administration demonstrates how to logon, track your portfolio, place a stock order, and view orders. Online trading is demonstrated in Figure 17-2.

Contact
Wall St Access @ www.wallstaccess.com

Figure 17-3

WALL ST ACCESS seeks to provide premium brokerage services at discount prices for the sophisticated trader. Their motto is "We fight for the extra 1/16 on every trade." Wall St Access offers a guarantee that if you are not satisfied with the service they will gladly refund the commission on any trade. Wall St Access' online trading demonstration is well featured and provides an excellent illustration of how online trading & investing work, Figure 17-3.

With these demonstrations you should have a foundation in online trading and investing. If you choose to trade online or purchase securities through an online service, be selective, and use the knowledge you have gained from the materials presented in Fell's Official Know-It-All Guide to Online Investing to Invest wisely in the New Millennium.

Contact
Ameritrade *@ www.ameritrade.com*

Figure 17-4

Ameritrade offers an express application which permits online trading the same market day. The application can be completed online and then it is submitted by US Mail or fax, Figure 17-4.

Contact
Brown & Company *@ www.brownco.com*

Figure 17-5

Brown & Company has certain requirements that must be met before they will service the Investor. These include at least five years of investment experience, $40,000 a year in net income, and a net worth of $50,000 exclusive of family residence. You must open the account with a minimum of $15,000 in cash or securities, Figure 17-5.

Contact
Charles Schwab @ *www.schwab.com*

Figure 17-6

Charles Schwab It takes a while to navigate the Schwab website to get to the nuts and bolts of opening an account. Once you do get there, you discover they require a minimum of $5,000 to open the account and fees from $0 to $25 per quarter depending on account balance with waivers. This is for the Schwab account. The Schwab One account requires a minimum deposit of $10,000, Figure 17.6.

Contact
Datek Online @ *www.datek.com*

Figure 17-7

Datek Online requires the completion of a secure online application to open an account with them. The signed application is returned by mail and the account is then funded, Figure 17-7.

Contact
CSFBdirect @ *www.csfbdirect.com*

Figure 17-8

DLJ Direct offers a paperless application for Individual, Joint and Custodial Accounts there is no need to send follow-up paperwork as the entire process is now online, Figure 17-8..

Contact
National Discount Brokers @
www.ndb.com

National Discount Brokers | ndb.com

Figure 17-9

National Discount Brokers has an online application which permits investors to commence trading in as little as 48 hours. You can also request a new account kit which is sent via US Mail. You may also visit their Retirement Center for IRA accounts, Figure 17-9.

Contact
TD Waterhouse @ *www.tdwaterhouse.com*

Figure 17-10

TD Waterhouse accounts are initiated online and are then followed up with signed applications. There are many types of accounts that TD Waterhouse handles for the Investor including Individual, Custodial, Business and Retirement Accounts among a number of others, Figure 17-10.

Chapter Eighteen

THE
21st CENTURY
INVESTOR

There are well in excess of 100 websites featured and illustrated in *Fell's Official Know-It-All Guide to Online Investing*. The intent of the Guide is to introduce investors and industry professionals to 21st Century Wall Street.

Having completed *Fell's Official Know-It-All Guide to Online Investing's* cyber-tour, you emerge a 21st Century Investor, ready to take control of your personal portfolio.

The knowledge you now have gives you tremendous power to make wise investment choices now and throughout the 21st Century. The 21st Century Investor has emerged, leaving all others in Cyber-dust.

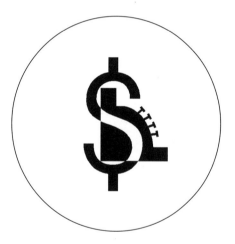

Web Addresses
By Alphabet

WEB ADDRESSES BY ALPHABET

A

4Annuities.Com
www.4annuities.com
ABC News.Com
www.abcnews.go.com
About.Com
www.about.com
Address.com
www.address.com
America Online www.aol.com
American Express Financial Advisors www.americanexpress.com
American Express Online Brokerage www.americanexpress.com
American Stock Exchange www.amex.com

WEB ADDRESSES BY ALPHABET

A

Annuities Online www.annuitiesonline.com
Apple www.corporate-ir.net
Ariel Mutual funds.Com* www.arielmutualfunds.com
Ask Research www.askresearch.com
AT&T WorldNet www.att.com

B

Barchart.com * www.barchart.com
Barron's Online www.interactive.wsj.com
BigCharts www.bigcharts.com
BigPlayStocks.com * www.bigplaystocks.com
Bloomberg.com * www.bloomberg.com
Blue Light.com * www.bluelight.com
Board of Trade Clearing Corporation www.botcc.com
Boston Stock Exchange www.bostonstock.com
Briefing.Com * www.briefing.com
Bureau of Public Debt www.publicdebt.treas.gov
BusinessWeek Online www.businessweek.com

WEB ADDRESSES BY ALPHABET

C

Chicago Board of Trade www.cbot.com
Chicago Board Options Exchange www.cboe.com
Chicago Mercantile Exchange www.cme.com
Chicago Stock Exchange www.chicagostockex.com
Citicorp Investment Services www.citibank.com
CNBC.com * www.cnbc.com
CNNfn.com * www.cnnfn.com
Commodities & Futures Trading Commission www.cftc.gov
Companies Online www.companiesonline.com
Compaq www.compaq.com
CompuServe www.compuserve.com
CPMnet www.cmpnet.com

D

Daily Graphs Online www.dailygraphs.com
Dell www.dell.com
dotNow www.dotnow.com
Dun & Bradstreet www.dnbcorp.com

WEB ADDRESSES BY ALPHABET

E

Epson www.epson.com
E*Trade www.etrade.com
Excite www.excite.com

F

Fannie Mae www.fanniemae.com
Federal Reserve Board www.bog.frb.fed.us
Fidelity Investments www.300.fidelity.com
FinanceWise www.financewise.com
Findafund.com * www.findafund.com
First Call Corporation www.firstcall.com
Forbes.com * www.forbes.com
Fortune www.fortuneinvestor.com
Freddie Mac www.freddiemac.com
Freei.net www.freeinet.com
Fujitsu www.fujitsu.com

WEB ADDRESSES BY ALPHABET

F

FinanceWise www.financewise.com
Findafund.com * www.findafund.com
First Call Corporation www.firstcall.com
Forbes.com * www.forbes.com
Fortune www.fortuneinvestor.com
Freddie Mac www.freddiemac.com
Freei.net www.freeinet.com
Fujitsu www.fujitsu.com

G

Gateway www.gateway.com
GE Financial Network www.getn.com
Ginnie Mae www.ginniemae.gov
Good Morning Silicon Valley www.mercurycenter.com
Google www.google.com
GoTo.Com * www.goto.com
Great Picks.Com * www.great-picks.com

WEB ADDRESSES BY ALPHABET

H

Hewlett Packard www.pandi.hp.com
HotBot www.hotbot.com

I

IBM www.ibm.com
iFreedom.com * www.ifreedom.com
ino.com * www.ino.com

J

Juno www.juno.com
Just Quotes.Com * www.justquotes.com

WEB ADDRESSES BY ALPHABET

K

Kiplinger.com * www.kiplinger.com

L

LookSmart www.looksmart.com
Los Alamos National Bank www.lanb.com

M

Market Guide Investor www.marketguide.com
MCI WorldCom * www.mciworld.com
Microsoft www.microsoft.com
MindSpring www.mindspring.com
Money.Com * www.pathfinder.com
Morgan Stanley Dean Witter Online www.online.msdw.com

WEB ADDRESSES BY ALPHABET

M

Mr. Stock www.secure.mrstock.com
MSN MoneyCentral www.moneycentral.msn.com
Muni Direct www.munidirect.com
Mutual funds Online www.mutualfundsnet.com

N

Nasdaq www.nasdaq.com
National Association of Securities Dealers www.nasd.com
Netscape www.netscape.com
Net Zero www.netzero.com
New York Board of Trade www.nybot.com
New York Merchantile Exchange www.nymex.com
New York Stock Exchange www.nyse.com

WEB ADDRESSES BY ALPHABET

O

Online Investor www.investhelp.com
OptionInvestor.com * www.optioninvestor.com
OptionsSource.com * www.optionsource.com
OTC Bulletin Board www.otcbb.com

P

Philadelphia Stock Exchange www.phlx.com
Prodigy Internet www.prodigy.com

WEB ADDRESSES BY ALPHABET

Q

QuickQuote.com
www.quickquote.com

R

Reuters www.reuters.com
Reuters moneynet www.moneynet.com

S

Sallie Mae www.salliemae.com
S&P Personal Wealth www.personalwealth.com
ScotTTrade www.scottrade.com
Securities & Exchange Commission www.sec.gov
Silicon Investor www.siliconinvestor.com
Snap www.snap.com
Sofcom * www.sofcom.com

WEB ADDRESSES BY ALPHABET

<u>S</u>

Sony www.sony.com
StockMaster.com * www.stockmaster.com
Stockselector.com*www.stockselector.com
Stocksmart.Com * www.stocksmart.com
StockTools www.financialweb.com

<u>T</u>

TechStockInvestor www.techstockinvestor.com
The Economist www.economist.com
The Free-PC Network www.free-pc.com
The Street.Com * www.thestreet.com
TIAA-CREF www.tiaa-cref.org

WEB ADDRESSES BY ALPHABET

U

USA Today Money www.usatoday.com

V, W

Wall St Access www.wsaccess.com
Wall Street Journal Interactive www.public.wsj.com
world spy.com
www.worldspy.com

X, Y, Z

Yahoo! Finance www.biz.yahoo.com
Zacks Investment Research www.zacks.com

Web Addresses
By Topic

<u>WEB ADDRESSES BY TOPIC</u>

Annuities & CDs

4Annuities.Com -- www.4annuities.com
American Express Financial Advisors -- www.americanexpress.com
Annuities Online --www.annuitiesonline.com
GE Financial Network -- www.getn.com
Los Alamos National Bank -- www.lanb.com
TIAA-CREF -- www.tiaa-cref.org
QuickQuote.com -- - www.quickquote.com

Computers

Apple -- www.corporate-ir.net
Compaq -- www.compaq.com
Dell -- www.dell.com
Fujitsu -- www.fujitsu.com
Gateway -- www.gateway.com
Hewlett Packard -- www.pandi.hp.com
IBM -- www.ibm.com
Microsoft -- www.microsoft.com
Sony -- www.sony.com

WEB ADDRESSES BY TOPIC

Exchanges (Futures)

Board of Trade Clearing Corporation -- www.botcc.com
Chicago Board of Trade -- www.cbot.com
Chicago Mercantile Exchange -- www.cme.com

Exchanges (Futures)

New York Board of Trade -- www.nybot.com
New York Merchantile Exchange -- www.nymex.com

Exchanges (Stock & Option)

American Stock Exchange -- www.amex.com
Boston Stock Exchange -- www.bostonstock.com
Chicago Board Options Exchange -- www.cboe.com
Chicago Stock Exchange -- www.chicagostockex.com
New York Stock Exchange -- www.nyse.com
Philadelphia Stock Exchange -- www.phlx.com
Nasdaq -- www.nasdaq.com
OTC Bulletin Board -- www.otcbb.com

WEB ADDRESSES BY TOPIC

Financial Analysis

Ask Research -- www.askresearch.com
Barchart.com -- - www.barchart.com
BigCharts -- www.bigcharts.com
Daily Graphs Online -- www.dailygraphs.com
StockMaster.com -- - www.stockmaster.com
StockTools -- www.financialweb.com

Financial News Services

ABC News.Com -- www.abcnews.go.com
CNBC.com -- www.cnbc.com
CNNfn.com -- www.cnnfn.com
Money.Com -- www.pathfinder.com
Reuters www.reuters.com
The Street.Com -- www.thestreet.com
USA Today Money -- www.usatoday.com
Wall Street Journal Interactive -- www.public.wsj.com

WEB ADDRESSES BY TOPIC

Financial Research Services

Briefing.Com -- www.briefing.com

Companies Online www.companiesonline.com

Dun & Bradstreet www.dnbcorp.com

FinanceWise www.financewise.com

First Call Corporation www.firstcall.com

Market Guide Investor www.marketguide.com

MSN MoneyCentral www.moneycentral.msn.com

Reuters moneynet www.moneynet.com

Zacks Investment Research www.zacks.com

Financial Webzines

Barron's Online www.interactive.wsj.com

BusinessWeek Online www.businessweek.com

Forbes.com -- www.forbes.com

Fortune www.fortuneinvestor.com

Kiplinger.com -- www.kiplinger.com

Online Investor www.investhelp.com

The Economist www.economist.com

WEB ADDRESSES BY TOPIC

Government Bonds & Agency Issues

Bureau of Public Debt www.publicdebt.treas.gov
Fannie Mae www.fanniemae.com
Freddie Mac www.freddiemac.com
Ginnie Mae www.ginniemae.gov
Muni Direct www.munidirect.com
Sallie Mae www.salliemae.com

Online Brokerage Firms & Trading Services

American Express Online Brokerage www.americanexpress.com
Citicorp Investment Services www.citibank.com
E*Trade www.etrade.com

WEB ADDRESSES BY TOPIC

Online Brokerage Firms & Trading Services

Fidelity Investments www.300.fidelity.com
Morgan Stanley Dean Witter Online www.online.msdw.com
Mr. Stock www.secure.mrstock.com
Quick & Reilly www.quick-reilly.com
ScotTTrade www.scottrade.com
Wall St Access www.wsaccess.com

Internet Service Providers

America Online www.aol.com
AT&T WorldNet www.att.com
CompuServe www.compuserve.com
MCI WorldCom -- www.mciworld.com
MindSpring www.mindspring.com
Prodigy Internet www.prodigy.com

WEB ADDRESSES BY TOPIC

Internet Service Providers (FREE)

Address.com -- www.address.com

Blue Light.com -- www.bluelight.com

dotNow www.dotnow.com

Freei.net www.freeinet.com

iFreedom.com -- www.ifreedom.com

Juno -- www.juno.com

Net Zero -- www.netzero.com

The Free-PC Network -- www.free-pc.com

world spy.com -- www.worldspy.com

Mutual Funds

American Express Financial Advisors -- www.americanexpress.com

Ariel Mutual funds.Com -- www.arielmutualfunds.com

Bloomberg.com -- www.bloomberg.com

Findafund.com -- www.findafund.com

Mutual funds Online -- www.mutualfundsnet.com

S&P Personal Wealth -- www.personalwealth.com

Yahoo! Finance -- www.biz.yahoo.com

WEB ADDRESSES BY TOPIC

Options

Bloomberg.com -- www.bloomberg.com
ino.com -- www.ino.com
OptionInvestor.com -- www.optioninvestor.com
OptionsSource.com -- www.optionsource.com
Stricknet.Com -- www.stricknet.com
Strikeprice.Com -- www.financialweb.com

Printers

Epson www.epson.com
Hewlett Packard www.pandi.hp.com

WEB ADDRESSES BY TOPIC

Regulators

Bureau of Public Debt -- www.publicdebt.treas.gov
Commodities & Futures Trading Commission -- www.cftc.gov
Federal Reserve Board -- www.bog.frb.fed.us
National Association of Securities Dealers -- www.nasd.com
Securities & Exchange Commission -- www.sec.gov

Stock

BigPlayStocks.com -- www.bigplaystocks.com
Great Picks.Com -- www.great-picks.com
Just Quotes.Com -- www.justquotes.com
Stocksmart.Com -- www.stocksmart.com
Stockselector.com -- www.stockselector.com

WEB ADDRESSES BY TOPIC

Stock (High Tech)

CPMnet -- www.cmpnet.com
Good Morning Silicon Valley -- www.mercurycenter.com
Silicon Investor -- www.siliconinvestor.com
Sofcom -- www.sofcom.com
TechStockInvestor -- www.techstockinvestor.com

Web Surfing

About.Com -- www.about.com
Excite -- www.excite.com
Google -- www.google.com
GoTo.Com -- www.goto.com
HotBot -- www.hotbot.com
LookSmart -- www.looksmart.com
Netscape -- www.netscape.com
Snap -- www.snap.com
Yahoo! -- www.yahoo.com

ONLINE GLOSSARIES

Alert IPO Dictionary -- *www.tradingday.com*

American Express Financial Advisors' Glossary -- *www.home.americanexpress.com*

Bank One Investment Glossary -- *www.oneinvest.com*

Bonds Online Glossary -- *www.bonds-online.com*

Brill's Funds Interactive Glossary -- *www.fundsinteractive.com*

Campbell R. Harvey's Hypertextual Finance Glossary -- *www.duke.edu*

CBS Marketwatch Glossary -- *www.wbs.marketwatch.com*

Chicago Board Options Exchange (CBOE) Glossary -- *www.cboe.*

Chicago Merchantile Exchange (CME) Glossary -- *www.cme.com*

CNNfn Glossary -- *www.cnnfn.com*

Commodities & Futures Trading Commission's Glossary -- *www.cftc.gov*

ONLINE GLOSSARIES

CompassWeb Brokerage Investment Glossary, -- *www.compassweb.com*

Consumer's Guide to Annuities, Annuity Guide, -- *www.galic.com*

DLJdirect's Investment Glossary, -- *www.dljdirect.com*

E-Muni Municipal Reading Room, Glossary, -- *www.emuni.com*

Equity Analytics, Glossary of Bond Terms, -- *www.e-analytics.com*

Federal Reserve Bank of Chicago Glossaries, -- *www.frbchi.org Federated*

Education Investment Glossary, -- *www.fedratedinvestors.com*

Fidelity Glossary, -- *www.wps.fidelity.com*

Finance Watch Glossary, -- *www.finance.wat.ch*

Glossary of Investment Terms, -- *www.greenjungle.com*

Investopaedia's Glossary, -- *www.buckinvestor.com*

Investor Resources Investment Glossary, -- *www.ai-investments-advice.com*

ONLINE GLOSSARIES

Investor Words Investing Glossary, -- *www.investorwords.com*

Investorama.com, Glossary, -- *www.investorama.com*

Investor's Galleria Glossary of Financial & Trading Terms, -- *www.centrex.com*

Lebenthal & Co Bond Terms, -- *www.cpateam.com*

Kiplinger Glossary -- *www.kiplinger.com*

KMS Financial Services Investment Glossary -- *www.kmsfinancial.com*

Money World's Glossary -- *www.moneyworld.com*

Moneyline.com Glossary -- *www.moneyline.com*

MoneyWords Glossary -- *www.jbu.edu*

Mutual Fund Glossary -- *www.fleet.com*

Nasdaq Glossary -- *www.nasdaq-amexnews.com*

NYSE Composite Indexes Glossary -- *www.stockcharts.com*

Quicken Glossary -- *www.quicken.com*

ONLINE GLOSSARIES

RBCO Investment Glossary -- *www.rbeck.com*

RLIG Investment Glossary -- *www.rlig.com*

Savoy Discount Brokerage Glossary -- *www.savoystocks.com*

SMG Glossary -- *www.phl.smginc.com*

The Digital Financier DFIN Glossary -- *www.dfin.com*

The Investment Club Glossary -- *www.investmentclub.about.com*

The Money Mentor's Glossary -- *www.moneymentor.com*

The Trader's Glossary -- *www.traders.com*

ThirdAge Investment Glossary -- *www.thirdage.com*

Thomson Investors Network, Fund Glossary -- *www.thomsoninvest.net*

Vanguard Group Glossary -- *www.vanguard.com*

Wall Street Directory Glossary -- *www.walstreetdirectory.com*

Washingtonpost.com Business Glossary -- *www.washintonpost.com*

Web Investors' Dictionary -- *www.webinvestors.com*

BIBLIOGRAPHY

1. About.Com, About Us, www.About.Com, 2000.

2. America Online, Who We Are, www.corp.aol.com, 2000.

3. American Express, About the Company, www.americanexpress.com, 2000

4. American Express Financial Advisors, Glossary--www.home.americanexpress.com,2000

5. American Stock Exchange, About Us, www.amex.com, 2000.

6. Apple, About Apple, www.corporate-ir.net, 2000.

7. Blue Light.com, About, www.bluelight.com, 2000.

8. Board of Trade Clearing Corporation, Who We Are, www.botcc.com, 2000.9

9. Boston Stock Exchange, What is a Stock Exchange?, www.bostonstock.com, 1997-1999

10. Boston Stock Exchange, Who We Are, www.boston stock.com, 1997-1999

11. Bureau of Public Debt, Online, www.publicdebt.treas.gov, 2000.

12. Chicago Board of Trade, About the Exchange, www.cbot.com, 2000.

13. Chicago Board Options Exchange, History, www.cboe.com, 2000.

14. Chicago Mercantile Exchange, About the Exchange, www.cme.com, 2000

BIBLIOGRAPHY

15. Chicago Stock Exchange, History, www.chicago stockex.com, 2000.

16. Commodities & Futures Trading Commission, About The Commission, www.cftc.gov, 2000.

17. Commodities & Futures Trading Commission, Glossary -- www.cftc.gov, 2000.

18. Compaq, About Us, www.compaq.com, 2000.

19. CompuServe, Corporate Information, www.compuserve.com, 2000.

20. Consumer's Guide to Annuities, Annuity Guide, www.galic.com, 2000.

21. Dell, About Dell, www.dell.com, 2000.

22. DLJdirect, Investment Glossary -- www.dljdirect.com, 2000.

23. Dotnow, About Us, www.dotnow.com, 2000. 24. 24. Dun & Bradstreet,

24. About D&B, www.dbncorp.com, 1999-2000.

25. Epson, Company Profile, www.epson.com, 1998.

26. E*Trade, The Story of E*Trade, www.etrade.com, 2000.

27. Fannie Mae, The Company, www.fanniemae.com, 2000.

28. Federal Reserve Board, Structure of the Federal Reserve System, www.bog.frb.fed.us,2000.

29. First Call, About First Call, www.1.firstcall.com, 2000.

30. Freddie Mac, About Freddie Mac, www.freddiemac.com, 2000.

31. Freei.net, About Us, www.freeinet.com, 2000.

32. Free-PC Network, About Us, www.free-pc.com, 2000.

33. Fujitsu, About Fujitsu, www.fjuitsu.com, 2000.

34. Gateway, About Us, www.gateway.com, 2000.

BIBLIOGRAPHY

35. Ginnie Mae, About Ginnie Mae, www.giniemae.com, 2000.

36. Google, Company Info, www.google.com, 2000.

37. GoTo.Com, Our Company, www.GoTo.com, 2000.

38. Hewlett Packard Company, Company Facts, www.hp.com, 1994-1999.

39. HotBot, Company Information, HotBot.lycos.com, 2000.

40. IBM Corporation, About IBM, www.ibm.com, 2000.

41. Internet Literacy, Fred T. Hofstetter, Irwin McGraw Hill 1998.

42. Investopaedia, Glossary -- www.buckinvestor.com, 2000.

43. Investor's Guide to Corporate Bonds, Understanding Collateralization, www.investingbonds.com, 2000.

44. Investorwords, Glossary -- www.investorwords.com, 2000.

45. Market Guide Investor, About, www.marketguide.com, 2000.

46. MCIworldcom, About The Company, www.wcom.com, 2000.

47. Microsoft Windows, Product Guide, www.microsoft.com, 2000.

48. MindSpring, About Us, www.mindspring.com, 2000.

49. Money World, Glossary -- www.moneyworld.com, 2000.

50. Morgan Stanley Dean Witter, Corporate Info, www.online.msdw.com, 2000.

51. Mutual funds Online, About Us, www.mfmag.com, 2000.

Notes...

Notes...

Notes...

Notes...

Notes...

Notes...

Notes...